Dedicated to *my darling wife Nicola.*

SURF KAYAKING THE ESSENTIAL GUIDE

By Simon Hammond

GREEN ROOM
PUBLISHING

First published in 2005 by **Green Room Publishing**.

Shoreline, Crooklets Beach, Bude, Cornwall, EX23 8NE

info@shorelineactivities.co.uk

Copyright © Simon Hammond 2005

ISBN-10: 0-9550520-0-9

ISBN-13: 978-0-95-505200-2

A CIP record for this book is available from the British Library

Designed by Samantha Taylor

Printed in England by Information Press 01865 882588

Distributed in Europe by Cordee Ltd www.cordee.co.uk

CONTENTS

Foreword

"Beautiful layout, teaser quotes, and thoughtful descriptions open doors to possibilities of some amazing rides."

Note to self: load my kayak and go to the surf! That is the bottom line effect of this remarkable book. I've learned new tricks to shred up some long rides, and saved myself some aches and pains of doing it wrong.

The learning process in kayaking, particularly in the surf can be brutal. Early in my paddling career, I joined a group of friends in a diversion from our normal river habitat to try our hand at some ocean surf. From shore it didn't look so bad, but we were quickly humbled by waves that pounded us. We should have had a clue, from the beating we took getting outside the break. Despite our decent river skills, we were no match for the ocean power. We were taking the ugly trial and error approach to learning.

Paddling is so much fun that it is easy to miss the opportunity to improve. I suppose some people prefer "the school of hard knocks", but really there is no excuse in today's sport. This "Essential Guide" is indeed that: an important shortcut to learning what you need to know.

With a few hours of reading you can eliminate years of trial and error and bad habits, and build a solid foundation of skills. You will be able to attack the wave with a clear concept of stability and well placed strokes. You'll gain genuine insight into how to pick the waves for a best ride, and develop tools to take off and ride them reliably. Then it gets fun. Beautiful layout, teaser quotes, and thoughtful descriptions open doors to possibilities of some amazing rides.

Pick up this book and you'll be longing for your next ride. A few thousand miles of surfable coastlines await us, with several waves a minute.
What are we waiting for?

Kent Ford
USA
www.performancevideo.com

Why should you read this book?

"There's no other sport that's so addictive. Whether it's the buzz, the fear, the speed or the beauty of surfing, once you've caught your very first wave you'll be hooked."

When I started to surf kayak I swam a lot! My boat was so heavy I could hardly carry it down the beach, my nylon spraydeck leaked like a sieve and my life-jacket filled with water. My first rides were chaotic and very short. The only thing I understood about "edge" was that when it snagged in the water the kayak would flip and I would be swimming. I loved it!

There's no other sport that's so addictive. Whether it's the buzz, the fear, the speed or the beauty of surfing, once you've caught your very first wave you'll be hooked. I was lucky: I lived by the sea, had boats I could borrow and friends to share those early faltering beginnings. My enthusiasm never waned and despite having no idea of how to surf I ploughed on regardless.

It took years to figure it all out. My progress was patchy, often stagnant, full of dead ends and wrong turns. In time I acquired a mixed array of skills and techniques, some of which were good, others poor and others that were plain old dangerous! Although I loved every unexpected minute of it I can't help but think how much faster I'd have picked up the essential skills of surfing if only I'd had some advice or guidance.

Since those early days I've been lucky enough to learn from some great surfers and my surfing has improved. I've surfed around the world on skis and in every type of kayak you can think of, I've been coached and I've spent a lot of time reflecting on my own skills and again my surfing has improved. Six months after winning the World Championships I finally figured out pre-rotation and my surfing improved again!

Anyone can improve their surfing at any stage of their development and from a multitude of sources. This book is just one possible source. In writing it I've tried to break the skills and knowledge of the sport down into sensible sections, from the basics to the advanced. You could read it from start to finish or just focus on the section that currently interests you. My hope is that as you read a section you'll develop thoughts and pictures in your head that will advance your knowledge and improve your surfing skills. I know you'll love the sport; I hope you'll enjoy the book.

GETTING STARTED

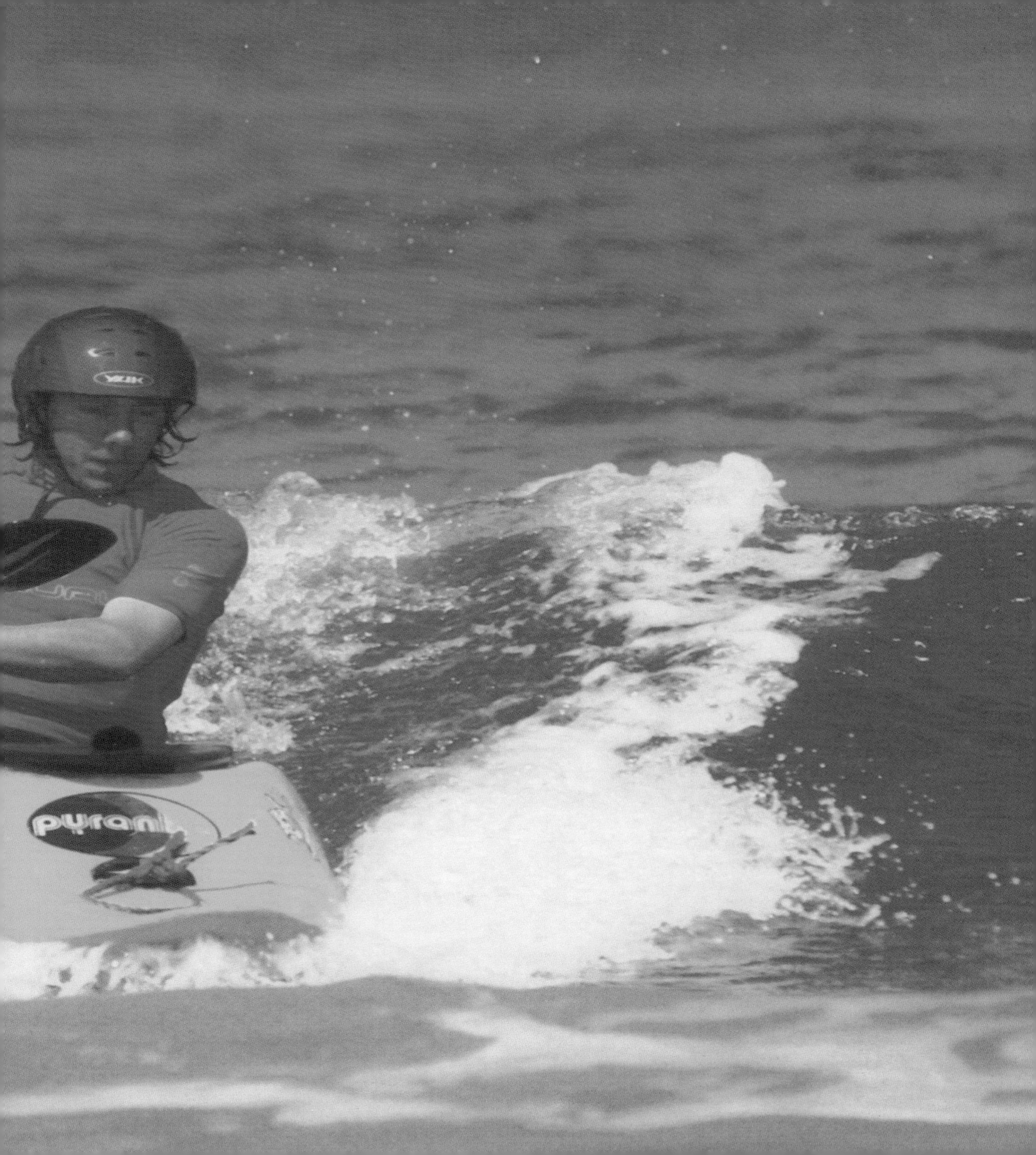

Introduction

One of the best things about this sport is that it's so easy to get started. Head for a safe sandy beach with a small amount of kit and some basic knowledge and away you go. Knowledge is the key and that's what this book is all about. But there are a few initial tips that will help you to get the most from your first surfing experience. In this chapter I'll try to put your mind at rest and give you the confidence to make a start. If you're asking yourself questions such as "Which boat is best for the surf? What extra kit do I need? Where and when should I surf? or How skilled do I need to be?" then read on.

Choosing the best boat

You can surf any make and model of kayak, surf ski or sit-on-top. Over the years I've seen surf skis and surf shoes, polo boats and slalom canoes, playboats, sit-on-tops and even inflatable boats used in the surfing environment. I've seen boats made out of plastic, fibreglass, epoxy and even wood. You could say "that as long as it floats it'll surf", which is true, but some boats lend themselves to the surfing environment more so than others.

The physical properties of a craft will affect the way it handles in the surf.

1. Very large and heavy craft are hard to handle in the surf and they're a real struggle to carry back up the beach at low tide. Some recreational sit-on-tops fall into this category and although they may have other good qualities, especially for the beginner, even the most inexperienced paddler should avoid the biggest and most cumbersome of models.

2. Longer boats may be less manoeuvrable than ultra short playboats but they'll have the speed necessary to catch a wave. For any surfer it's very demoralising to be out in the surf struggling to catch a single wave. Remember that when you're trying to catch a wave boat length equals speed and without speed you'll have a hard time catching waves. Choose a reasonably long kayak over an ultra short playboat.

3. Rocker has a huge effect on how a craft moves through the water and hence how it surfs. Rocker is the amount the craft bends up at its bow and stern. Lots of rocker at the bow will help to stop the craft from nose diving or pearling during the take-off. It will also help guide the craft up and over the oncoming waves during the paddle out, definitely a positive surfing feature.

Rocker at the stern has a negative effect. It increases drag and slows the craft down as it surfs across the wave. High performance surf kayaks and surf skis have hardly any rocker at the stern, allowing these craft to travel at very high speeds. This is a great feature for the experienced surfer but other design features can make these craft difficult to surf for those new to the sport.

4. The cross-sectional profile of the craft has huge effects on how it surfs, particularly the shape of the hull and the sides of the craft. Rounded hulls and sides are very forgiving and therefore ideal for the novice surfer. However as you gain a feel for the surf a more rectangular profile provides some very useful features. The sharper edge created between a flat hull and vertical sides allows a craft to carve tighter turns and to hold its edge more efficiently when travelling across the sloping face of a wave. Playboats usually have this flat hull, sharp edge design which also gives them the ability to flat spin. Playboats aren't primarily designed for surfing and their very positive hull and edge features can often be impaired by having a short overall length and a high degree of stern rocker.

5. Overall stability varies from craft to craft and is not just a result of width. Wider craft are certainly more stable, if a little slower, but the shape of the hull, height of the seat and the shape, length and volume of the stern all have an effect. Surf skis are particularly difficult to balance on due to their low overall volume, narrow width, high seat position and short tail. Even experienced surfers will sit astride their surf skis whilst waiting for a wave rather than try to balance in a proper paddling position.

6. Lots of volume may make the craft extremely buoyant but from a surfing point of view it makes the craft prone to getting trapped by a white water wave. The more volume a craft has, the more there is of it to be pushed around by the wave - it's harder to punch out through large oncoming waves and harder to pull off a wave once it's broken. Less volume in the stern of the craft helps to produce a sharp edge and a knife like tail that gives the craft a much greater level of manoeuvrability.

"Even experienced surfers will sit astride their surf skis whilst waiting for a wave rather than try to balance in a proper paddling position."

"Fit airbags in any rear spaces to stop the kayak from completely filling with water when you capsize"

The right kit

Wearing a tight fitting neoprene spraydeck is the best way to keep water out of your kayak whilst you're paddling out through the surf but a nylon deck will be easier to get off in a hurry. Be careful not to buy a spraydeck that is too tight. You'll need to be able to launch yourself from the water's edge without anyone else to help and an over tight spraydeck can make this impossible.

Surfers tend to use fairly short paddles of less than two metres in total length. Short paddles allow for rapid acceleration whilst paddling out and when catching a wave. They also have the advantage of being less cumbersome whilst surfing. Paddles need to be strong; remember that an aluminium shaft will be very cold to touch in the winter and is eventually corroded by salt water.

A kayaking helmet gives much better forehead protection than a surfer's helmet. A helmet is essential when you're learning as there is always the chance of your boat being washed over you after a capsize. I'd always recommend wearing a helmet when surfing in a large group, when surfing near rocks or in very shallow conditions.

Buoyancy aids have more use that just keeping you afloat. If it's a good fit it'll help to keep you warm and will also help to keep your spraydeck sealed tight around your torso. A smooth sleek buoyancy aid will cause a lot less drag when paddling out through the surf than a multi-pocketed, high buoyancy version.

Your paddling clothes are down to you but my advice is always to dress expecting to take a swim. In the summer months you may be able to get away with shorts and a rash vest but some additional layers will make your surfing session much more enjoyable. Wetsuits are buoyant, warm and good for swimming but can be a little restrictive around the shoulders. A wetsuit will keep you warm but you'll still get chilled when it's windy so in these conditions add a basic wind proof jacket as a top layer. Fleeces and dry suits are warmer than wetsuits (sometimes too warm) but nowhere near as good for active swimming.

Finally, fit the kayak out with tails of rope or tape at either end to grab onto when you capsize. Fit airbags in any rear spaces to stop the kayak from completely filling with water when you capsize and ensure it has a good solid footrest. If you have a surf ski then consider fitting a surf leash to avoid it being washed away when you come off.

Finding a good place to surf

For someone who lives inland the coastline may seem like a fairly uniform divide between the land and sea. Involve yourself in any coastal pursuit and you'll soon find out that this couldn't be further from the truth.

There are two basic features that affect a coastline's suitability for surfing. The first is its structure or morphology and the second is its global position relative to a good source of ocean swell.

Some coastlines just don't lend themselves to surfing: take the vertical cliffs along the Great Australian Bight plummeting directly into the ocean, or an extensive mud flat associated with an estuary. Ideal surfing coastlines will have some feature that slopes gently into the ocean: a sandy beach, a rock ledge or a coral reef for example. The steeper or more sudden the slope the higher the energy of the breaking wave. A newcomer to surfing would be well advised to surf on gently sloping sandy beaches where there is every chance of finding easy to ride spilling waves, perfect for developing good technique. Sandy beaches are relatively easy to launch from, they are often easy to gain access to and in many parts of the world they are the focus for the local surfing and life guarding community from which valuable information and advice can be gained.

Not every sandy beach, rocky ledge or coral reef gets great surf. A coastline needs to be in just the right global position in order for the ocean to deliver a good quality, consistent swell. Swell is generated by wind passing over large stretches of water and so it follows that a coastline facing out over a large ocean will get its fair share of surf. Most surfers will use some sort of guide book to steer them to the best locations. Guide books are a great help and a very worthwhile investment.

"Ideal surfing coastlines will have some feature that slopes gently into the ocean."

"The prevailing wind, weather and temperature will all have an effect on your surfing experience."

How conditions change
with the seasons

Even in classic surf locations, like Hawaii, the surf doesn't stay the same all year round. As the seasons change so do the atmospheric pressure systems. The prevailing wind, weather and temperature will all have an effect on your surfing experience.

The Summer.
Good weather, light winds, warm water and small surf. Not a bad environment for your very first go but beware the crowds. When the surf zone gets packed, tempers can fray.

The Autumn.
Still good weather over the land but a better chance of swell generating winds in the mid-ocean. The water is still at its summer temperature but the surf is usually bigger and much more consistent. This is a great time to go surfing.

The Winter.
Depends on where in the world you are but winter weather can be extreme with gales or very low temperatures. Often lots of big surf being generated which can be spoilt by high speed on-shore winds. However when the winds are light or off-shore this is the time of year to get in the water and surf the biggest of swells, not the time of year for your first session.

The Spring.
Improving weather but the water is still very cold. Mid-ocean storms still generating good swell. Like the autumn, a good time to surf before the swell drops off and the crowds build up in the summer.

How skilled do I need to be?

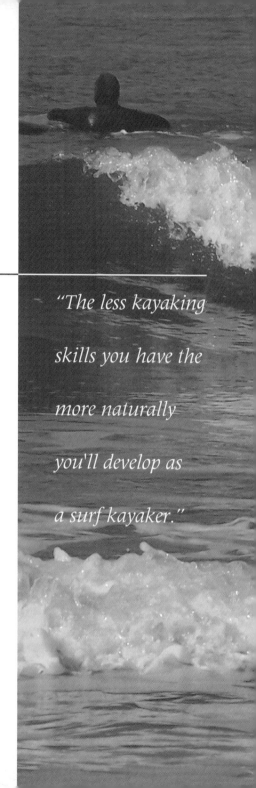

The answer is you don't need to be a skilled kayaker at all. In fact you could argue that the less kayaking skills you have the more naturally you'll develop as a surf kayaker. If your kayaking skills are advanced then you'll just need to focus on adapting your techniques to the surfing environment, and vice versa if you're already into surfing your focus will be on developing sound kayaking skills.

There are some fundamental kayaking skills that will enhance your first session in the surf. Being able to get out of your kayak safely after a capsize is probably number one and worth practising either before or at the very beginning of your first session. It's a skill you'll need almost straight away! Other than that, being comfortable in your craft and able to paddle in a reasonably straight line are the minimum requirements.

Some people see surf kayaking as a difficult sport and one that needs a high level of competency in order to be safe. This isn't true. As long as you surf within your limits you can have hours of fun developing your surfing and kayaking skills as you go. If you've the opportunity to develop your kayaking skills away from the surf then there are plenty of possibilities around the world where you can receive quality kayak coaching using well established coaching schemes such as the British Canoe Union's star awards.

"The less kayaking skills you have the more naturally you'll develop as a surf kayaker."

"Almost any type of kayak, ski or sit-on top will be good enough to get you started and the sooner you start surfing the better."

Summary

There really aren't many barriers to stop you from surf kayaking. Almost any type of kayak, surf ski or sit-on-top will be enough to get you started and when it comes to making choices about which craft to buy or borrow remember the key variables: length, rocker and cross-sectional profile. These will determine how the craft performs in the surfing environment. As far as what to wear is concerned, make it safe and comfortable and above all else dress expecting to take a swim!

Suitable surfing locations can be found all around the world but even at the top spots the size and consistency of the surf will vary throughout the seasons. If you only ever buy one other surfing book then buy a surf guide: it'll save you lots of time and will pin point locations that match your ability, whatever that might be.

* Long kayaks will catch waves much more easily than short kayaks.

* Lots of stern rocker creates drag which slows you down when surfing across a wave.

* A kayak with sharp edges and a flat hull will perform well in the surf but can be unforgiving for a beginner.

* A neoprene spraydeck, short paddles, a good helmet, sleek buoyancy aid and a flexible wetsuit are a useful guide for what to wear but there are plenty of other possibilities.

* Buy a surf guide to help pin point the best surfing locations but take into account how the surf and weather will vary throughout the year.

* Don't worry about your kayaking or surfing skills. The sooner you start surf kayaking the better.

* Knowledge is more important than equipment, so read on!

SAFE SURFING

Introduction

Safe surfing is more than just looking after yourself: it's about protecting the safety of other surfers and water users, and it's about knowing your limits and how to act in different situations. It sounds so obvious and yet, because surfing is so different from many other paddling environments, it's easy to make mistakes.

When I started to surf I was young and knew nothing, but that was OK because I also couldn't paddle! I was forced to stay in the shallows, surfing white water waves; not because I particularly wanted to but because I couldn't get out the back. During this apprenticeship I picked up the do's and don'ts, I started to appreciate the power of the surf and as I started to venture further out I learnt about the road rules and etiquette.

If you haven't got time for the full apprenticeship then my advice is learn as much as you can before you take to the water and then be cautious. It's the best way to make friends and gain respect.

The road rules

Taking off on a green wave and surfing straight towards the beach could be as risky as standing on the hard shoulder of a motorway and walking towards the central reservation. You might be lucky but then again you might be the cause of a horrendous collision.

Unlike rivers the ocean has a considerable amount of width and it's this width that is exploited by the surfing community. Given the chance a surfer would never end up on the beach as the perfect wave would just go on for ever with the surfer continually slicing across its face until exhaustion marked the end of the ride.

The reality, when surfing off a sandy beach, is that no matter how fast or far a surfer travels across a wave they will also be travelling towards the shore and it's this that creates the confusion. Surfing towards the beach is an unlucky coincidence rather than the primary aim.

Primary direction of travel on the green face of a wave is parallel to the beach rather than towards it. Once the wave breaks, direction of travel becomes more erratic and for many experienced surfers finishes altogether. This now becomes the zone of the novice surfer, belly boarder and swimmer where riding each wave a safe distance apart is of greater importance than which direction the wave is surfed.

"Primary direction of travel on the green face of a
wave is parallel to the beach rather than towards it."

Surf etiquette

Surfing etiquette is all about maintaining a safe and chilled out surfing environment. It's true to say that many of the hard rules of surfing etiquette have their greatest relevance when applied to surfing peeling green waves but even when surfing white water waves etiquette and consideration for other water users will ensure a pleasant experience for everyone.

The golden rule. Never drop in. Dropping in has got to be the biggest, most common, most annoying and potentially most dangerous mistake in the surf. It's guaranteed to lose you friends instantly and labels you a t*@*t! for the rest of the session. But the thing is, it's an easy mistake to make. So what is it and how can you avoid it.

"Dropping in has got to be the biggest, most common, most annoying and potentially most dangerous mistake in the surf."

Dropping in is quite simply dropping down the green face of a wave in front of an oncoming surfer. They may have been surfing across the wave for ages or have caught it a split second before you; it doesn't matter. The crime is still the same and it's well worth avoiding.

It happens because people don't check the wave before they catch it. A driver wouldn't dream of joining the flow of traffic before checking up and down the road and ultimately giving way if required, yet this type of common sense is often absent in the surf.

The key is to recognise who has the right of way and that's not too hard. Give way to any surfer who has caught the wave way before you or to a surfer who is closer to the peeling lip of the wave and therefore in a more critical and possibly more vulnerable position. There are always going to be grey situations which can be best resolved at the time with good communication and a non-aggressive attitude. No wave is worth upsetting someone, let alone injuring them. Most of the rest of the rules of etiquette are just common sense but still worth mentioning.

When you paddle out through the surf avoid surfers riding the incoming waves. On point breaks and reef breaks the surfing line is well defined and it's easy to avoid the wave riding surfers by paddling out away from the powerfully breaking waves, using rips and deep water channels to your benefit. However on beach breaks or when a collision looms near it's the paddling out surfer who needs to get out of the way even if this means taking a big white water hit, better that than spoiling someone's wave or actually causing an accident.

This paddle out rule also impacts on some of the surf kayakers more extreme manoeuvres, especially manoeuvres done as the wave breaks or on white water waves. For a paddling out surf boarder there is often nothing more bewildering than the flat spin or cartwheel. They just don't know where you're going and so have trouble choosing their own anti-collision route past you. Try to understand it from their position and perhaps avoid alarming moves (that may look like you're out of control) in front of those paddling out.

Know your limits. When I first started surf kayaking one thing above all else became very clear. It's a lot easier to be in control when you paddle out than being in control when you surf back in. It's not the same on a board as newcomers to the sport rarely have the skills or strength to paddle very far out to start with. To know your limits takes experience and we all make mistakes; it's just that in kayaks we've got the potential to make really big mistakes! When you surf a new break take it easy, take some time assessing the conditions before going in, don't get caught out by a set wave before you've ridden a few smaller swells and in order to have the most enjoyable experience try to surf in the conditions that best match your ability.

Don't hog waves. Just because you can paddle out faster than boogie boarders and board riders, don't take more than your fair share of waves. It's especially important when the waves are in limited supply and there's a large number of surfers in the water. It's not a life or death rule but it's a way of making friends rather than enemies.

Snaking may well be OK in a competition but it's too aggressive in a friendly, mellow free-surfing session. So what is snaking? Basically it's a definite, sudden and often disguised change of position that gives the snaker right of way for the next wave. You can understand why it's part of competition but this sort of behaviour is out of order in a recreational setting.

In competition, etiquette gets pushed to the limit.

Who has right of way on this wave?

Lifeguards and flags

There are plenty of beaches and breaks where you'll never see a lifeguard but if you're surfing off a lifeguarded beach anywhere in the world it's useful to know how to be in harmony with them and their systems.

Lifeguards come in all shapes and forms, with all sorts of personalities, attitudes and opinions. In different parts of the world they are employed by the police force, fire service, coastguard, local authority, lifeboat organisations or are trained volunteers. Like them or not they do represent a great source of local knowledge and you'd be a fool to ignore their advice. If you're surfing somewhere new take the initiative and go and have a chat. Be honest about your intentions, interests and ability and in return you'll end up with some valuable information and a useful contact.

The most obvious signs of a lifeguarded or patrolled beach are the flags. A world wide system ensures that this doesn't get too complicated.

A pair of **red and yellow flags** are used to designate a safe swimming area. This is clearly the no-go-area for any surf craft other than belly boards. That's fine except for the fact that the very water features lifeguards use to define a safe swimming area are often exactly what a surfer is looking for. If this is the case then you've some very limited options.

1. Look for another break or come back after 6 pm.
2. If the waves start to peel inside the swim zone but finish peeling out of its limits then you may be able to coexist without coming into contact with the swimmers themselves. However it's only going to take one wipe out or bongo slide and hey presto you'll be hurtling into unsuspecting bodies. You could end up causing some serious injuries, you'll be yet another example of a typical bloody goat boater and you'll have the resident lifeguard fraternity on your back for the rest of your trip. Definitely a high risk option.

A **black and white chequered flag** is used to denote the safe area for surf craft, which includes kayaks, skis, boards and competent boogie boarders. It's not always used and it might not be the only place on a beach for such craft to surf. If in doubt ask the lifeguards.

A **red flag** is used to denote dangerous conditions. Who it's aimed at however is a bit ambiguous. On two beaches in North Cornwall just 3 miles apart it has two very different meanings. On one beach it means this beach is closed for swimmers but is safe enough for surfers, whilst on the other beach it means this beach is too dangerous for anyone to enter the water. Again you're best to check with the lifeguards.

"The most obvious signs of a lifeguarded or patrolled beach are the flags"

NORTH CORNWALL DISTRICT COUNCIL

TYPICAL CURRENTS OFF A BEACH

RIP CURRENTS   RIP CURRENTS

CALM WATER

DANGEROUS BATHING

MALIBU BOARDS CANOES AND WINDSURFING AREA

BATHING AREA INCLUDING BELLY & BOOGIE BOARDS

| ALWAYS CHOOSE A SPOT WHERE THE WAVES ARE ROLLING EVENLY TO SHORE | DO NOT BATHE WHERE THE WATER IS CALM. *(STILL WATERS RUN DEEP).* | IF CAUGHT IN A RIP CURRENT, SWIM ACROSS IT, *NOT AGAINST IT.* |

BE SAFE   BE WISE   BE ALIVE

BE SAFE
- ✓ DO WAVE ARM FROM SIDE TO SIDE IF IN TROUBLE
- ✓ DO ALLOW AT LEAST 1 HOUR BETWEEN EATING AND SWIMMING
- ✓ DO OBSERVE THE FLAGS
- ✓ DO BE CONSIDERATE TO OTHER USERS
- ✗ DON'T TAKE INFLATABLES INTO THE SEA
- ✗ DON'T LEAVE SMALL CHILDREN UNSUPERVISED
- ✗ DON'T SIT ON ROCKS WHERE LARGE WAVES BREAK
- ✗ DON'T SWIM ALONE

BE WISE

RED FLAG MEANS DANGER
DO NOT ENTER THE WATER TO BATHE

BE ALIVE
- ✗ DON'T PICK UP UNIDENTIFIED OBJECTS
- ✗ DON'T DRINK ALCOHOL AND THEN SWIM
- ✗ DON'T STAY IN THE SEA IF YOU GET COLD
- ✗ DON'T USE MOTORISED CRAFT FROM HERE
- ✓ DO OBEY LIFEGUARDS
- ✓ DO SWIM ACROSS RIP CURRENT IF CAUGHT IN THEM
- ✓ CHECK TIDE TIMES AND BEWARE OF BEING STRANDED
- ✓ DO PUT LITTER IN BINS PROVIDED

EMERGENCY PHONE ☎ **AT LIFEGUARD HUT**
999

IN EMERGENCY INFORM THE LIFEGUARD

IF NO LIFEGUARD PHONE 999 FOR THE COASTGUARD

LIFEGUARDS ARE ON DUTY FROM END OF MAY TO MID SEPTEMBER FROM 10 am TO 6 pm

"Try to surf with others but don't get complacent. When things really go wrong, you're on your own."

In addition to knowing your etiquette, the road rules, and following any good local advice there's a few more things you can do to maximise your own safety.

Choose a safe beach to start with. Talk to surfing friends, use the internet or a good surf guide and choose a beach that matches your level of ability and experience. As a general rule most surfers would start surfing from sandy beaches before progressing to point breaks and reef breaks.

Try to surf with others but don't get complacent. Fellow kayakers or boardies may be able to help if you take a swim. They might be able to assist you in getting back in your boat or even tow you and your kit back to shore

When I do take a big hit and things are going wrong I try to take all factors into account before deciding on a course of action, and even then I'm always ready to change my plan as required.

Paddling a swamped boat back to the beach is often more effective than coming out completely and trying to tow it in. You could even have a go at surfing it back by lying on it like a surf board. If I am out of my boat then good end grabs or knotted tape gives me a chance to keep hold of it as breaking waves try to rip it out of my grasp. A river crab on a releasable waist belt gives me an option for somewhere to put my paddles so that I can use my arm(s) to assist with my swimming.

Self Safety

or away from hazards. Rely on others too much and you'll end up in trouble as when things really go wrong, you're on your own.

Make sure your equipment is as safe as possible. In many paddlesport disciplines you'll find the experts don't often take a swim but that's not so true when it comes to surfing!

When I go surfing I dress with the expectation of taking a swim. Sure I consider the warmth and comfort of my clothing but I also consider the amount of buoyancy my clothing will give me as well as how streamlined it is. I avoid the big and baggy and select the sleek. A taut, well fitting spraydeck minimises the times when a breaking wave causes it to implode. A boat full of buoyancy will stop it filling with water making it easier to tow back to the beach or paddle it back in a semi-swamped condition.

Swimming and dragging a boat in through the surf can at best be quick, simple and controlled, at other times full of risk and at others a long slog. A friend of mine, Bryce Barr, once took over an hour to swim back to the beach with his kayak having negotiated a complicated rip current, a breakwater and a line of rocks. In the fading light of evening he slogged it out, holding on to all his kit and on that occasion it was a good choice. At other times as I've been dragged relentlessly towards the rocks I've ditched my boat and paddles and used all my energy for self survival. It paid off; I wasn't hurt and nor in the end was my kit, although it took some time to find it!

There is no one correct answer, just make sure that you're prepared. You'll always take the odd swim but the chances are you'll spend more time rescuing others rather than being rescued yourself.

Summary

The surfing environment has its own limits of acceptable behaviour based on protecting the safety of fellow surfers and other water users. If you want to make friends and win respect then it's a good idea to know as much about these rules and etiquette as possible. The road rules give you a fundamental understanding of how to use the surf, which path you should be attempting to follow along a wave and where the traffic will be coming from. Good etiquette stops accidents, keeps you safe and wins you friends. Lifeguards and other authorities are a feature of many of our popular surfing beaches and although their systems can have an impact on our surfing their local knowledge and advice can be of great use. Having taken care of everyone else in the water don't forget to consider your own safety. What you wear, where you surf and what you do if things go wrong are all worth planning out. It's best to avoid an epic, but if you have one then it's best to be prepared.

* If you haven't got time for a full surfing apprenticeship then learn as much as you can before you take to the water and then be cautious.

* The primary direction of travel on the green face of a wave is parallel to the beach rather than towards it.

* Surfing etiquette is all about maintaining a safe and chilled out surfing environment.

* The golden rule is never drop in. Dropping in has got to be the biggest, most common, most annoying and potentially most dangerous mistake in the surf.

* The most obvious signs of a lifeguarded or patrolled beach are the flags. A world wide system ensures that this doesn't get too complicated.

* Make sure your equipment is as safe as possible. Always dress with the assumption that you'll take a swim.

* When things are going wrong assess your situation and be adaptable.

"Good etiquette stops accidents,
keeps you safe and wins you friends."

BUILDING STRONG FOUNDATIONS

"Good forward trim will push our bow down, decreasing drag and allowing us to accelerate once again"

Introduction

The problem with us paddlers is that on the whole we're lazy. Ask us to sit upright in our kayaks and what you actually get is a sort of rounded shoulders, slouched position. We're so used to this armchair-in-front-of-the-telly position that even state-of-the-art backrests do little to improve this poor posture.

But why is it bad posture and why when we're surfing is a good arched back and forward leaning body position the best? The answer is all about functional stability and trim. Getting these foundations right will transform a paddler from a weak, wobbling, edge tripping, drunk into a strong, stable, smooth surfing, sprinter. Sorry about the S's but do you get the picture? - THIS IS IMPORTANT.

Imagine you're sprinting along in a fast flat water racing K1. The K1 is slicing through the water, acting as a true displacement hulled craft. Your maximum speed is more or less set by the length of the boat but the effort needed to reach this maximum will be affected by trim. If you weight the boat too much to the back then it will sit tail down in the water, increasing drag so making it much harder for you to paddle fast.

Now imagine a speed boat accelerating as it leaves the harbour. Initially the speed boat sits in the water like our K1 but then as the power of the engine is increased the bow lifts as the boat climbs over its very own bow wave. This bow-high position creates lots of drag but the engine is strong enough to keep the boat accelerating until whoosh........ the boat climbs out of the water, breaks free from the drag of displacing water and starts to plane along the surface.

Now think about catching a wave. As we paddle to catch the wave it's as if we're in our K1, the length of our boat is setting our maximum speed and good forward trim will help to minimise drag. As we catch the wave and accelerate down its face we're now in the speed boat trying to break free from the water. Our bow lifts as we accelerate and drag starts to slow us down, but good forward trim will push our bow down, decreasing drag and allowing us to accelerate once again helping us to break free of the water and plane along down the face of the wave.

The truth about surf kayaking is that we haven't got an unlimited power supply. In fact, the power generated by surfing across the face of a wave is only just enough to get us up to a planing speed, most of the time we're in a semi-planing state just like the speed boat in its bow high position. This actually makes trim even more important, as it's only with good forward trim that we've any chance of keeping our bows down enough to ever break through the plane barrier.

Establishing functional stability

So leaning forwards in your kayak will increase your speed but it will also improve your functional stability and that's as important to a surf kayaker as it is to the winger in a rugby team.

Have you ever sat in your kayak sideways-on to the surf and let a wave just roll into you? You should try it. What happens? What happens if you do it again and this time take your paddles away? Who reckons they'll capsize? But on which side will you fall over, your beachward side or your seaward side? The answer is that with good functional stability you shouldn't capsize at all, even without the paddles. As paddlers we tend to substitute stability for support, with a set of paddles in our hands we're quite good at support and as a consequence we don't worry enough about stability.

So why are we like that winger in the rugby team? Well he too is going to get hit from the side, probably by the opposition's full back, but if he can stay on his feet as he's tackled he might still score the try. In our kayaks we're in a similar position; if we can stay upright and balanced as the wave hits us we'll stay in control and be able to continue our ride. The rugby player hasn't got a set of paddles for support so has to rely on functional stability to maintain his balance in the tackle, he doesn't buckle sideways towards the tackler or lean away from him, as in both cases he'd be off balance, he simply stays strong, he allows himself to be deflected but stays balanced, stays on his feet and scores the try. As the white water wave hits us from the side think like the rugby player. Don't collapse sideways towards it or lean away from it but be strong and maintain your balance as you take the hit.

Being strong in a sitting position isn't easy - we need to have a strong connection between our upper body and our legs which are firmly gripping the inside of our kayaks. We need to have a good fit inside our kayaks but the critical link is in our trunk, in fact a band of muscle that lies deep in our stomach. Slouch back and this muscle is useless. Roll your hips forwards and sit in a tall upright position and we can create a strong and powerful bond. This bond, together with the firm bracing of the kayak with our legs, is the basis of balance and allows the smooth transition of movement and power from our upper body through to our kayaks and vice versa.

Developing this functional stability is quite straightforward. Sit in your boat and let white water waves hit you from the side, play around with the size of the waves, the side they hit you, holding your paddles in one hand or give them to your buddy! Now try it leaning back in the old slumped position and you'll soon be converted to a good strong forward leaning body position!

"With good functional stability

you shouldn't capsize at all,

even without the paddles."

A momentary loss of edge awareness

can lead to all sorts of trouble

Developing edge awareness

All this talk of trim and functional stability is fine but if we're going to become really smooth surfers then we've got to start developing edge awareness. What the hell's edge awareness I hear you cry. Well in surfing terms it's knowing and being able to feel the difference between catching an edge, a skimming edge and a carving edge. And there's no better activity for developing this awareness than good old fashioned bongo sliding.

Bongo sliding, or being pushed sideways to the beach on a white water wave, is great - as long as there's no one beach side of you! Being pushed sideways towards the beach usually focuses paddlers' minds on controlling the amount of lift they give the beachward edge of your kayak.

You see in this position you're very much like a skimming stone, leading edge too high and the stone stalls. Beachward edge of our kayak too high and we stall, we get left behind as the wave continues towards the beach. Leading edge of the stone too low and the stone bites into the water and sinks. Beachward edge of our kayak too low and it bites into the still water in front of the wave, we catch an edge and are instantly flipped over. But when the leading edge of that stone is just right the stone will effortlessly skim over the water surface with hardly any resistance. When we hold the beachward edge of our kayaks at just the right angle we will skim along sideways with hardly any resistance, letting the wave push us smoothly to the shore.

Bongo sliding

Developing this feel for the edge of your kayak takes a little practice but it's worth it. All you need are some white water waves and a bit of space. Make sure that your feet, knees and thighs are in continuous contact with the kayak, adopt a good forward leaning body position and be strong. Catch a white water wave at a 45° angle and you'll find yourself instantly surfing sideways. Now focus on what you're doing inside your kayak. You'll lift the edge of your kayak by lifting or tensing one of your knees more than the other. Too much lift leads to too much edge; you'll create too much resistance for skimming and you'll come off the back of the wave. On each wave you catch you should decrease the amount you lift your beachward edge until you're skimming effortlessly towards the shore, decrease it a little more and you'll find out what it feels like to catch an edge (it's worth knowing, honest!).

Apart from a successful bongo slide why is a feel for a skimming edge so important? Well there are three very good reasons:

The creation of a reference point. It gives you a reference point for edging. Less edge leads towards catching-an-edge whilst more edge leads towards a carving edge.

You learn how to hold your kayak. You learn how to smoothly and firmly hold an edge with good muscular tension inside your kayak.

The basis for the pivot and skim top turn. Being able to set and feel a skimming edge is the key to the most widely used manoeuvre at the top of the wave, namely the pivot and skim top turn.

"All you need are some white water waves and a bit of space. Make sure that your feet, knees and thighs are in continuous contact with the kayak, adopt a good forward leaning body position and be strong."

"Sit in front of a few white water waves and let yourself get hit from the side, hold a strong forward leaning body position and stay balanced."

Summary

Without strong foundations you've no chance of building solid technique. It's easy to be impatient; the pull of a beautiful peeling green wave is an almost irresistible force. But before you head off hoping that, with luck, you might just have a good ride, give yourself a fighting chance. Be aware of your body position in your boat, think about how it affects trim and how this in turn affects the speed your boat will travel through the water. Sit in front of a few white water waves and let yourself get hit from the side, hold a strong forward leaning body position and stay balanced. Now actively catch a white water wave and let it bongo slide you back to the beach, experiment with different degrees of edge, find the limits, find the point where you're skimming with least resistance letting yourself get pushed right up to the shore. Now you're ready to go surfing.

* Ask a kayaker to sit upright and what you actually see is a sort of rounded shoulders, slouched position.

* Getting the foundations right will transform a paddler from a weak, wobbling, edge tripping, drunk into a strong, stable, smooth surfing, sprinter.

* As we speed up to catch a wave our bow lifts and drag starts to slow us down. Leaning forwards will push our bow back down so decreasing this drag effect.

* Being strong in a sitting position isn't easy. We need to have a good fit inside our kayaks and sit with our hips rolled forwards to generate good functional stability.

* To become really smooth surfers we've got to develop edge awareness.

* There's no better activity for developing edge awareness than good old fashioned bongo sliding.

MAXIMISING THE WHITE WATER WAVE

Introduction

All too often we ignore or miss opportunities to improve our surfing skills by not using white water waves on which to practise. Sure it's not the real thing, but there are so many skills that you can develop simply by surfing white water waves, that to ignore them is to lose out.

In addition there's no getting away from the fact that all waves will sooner or later break into a white water wave. In some situations continuing to surf a wave after it breaks would be considered reckless, dangerous or just a plain old waste of effort. Whilst at other times continuing to surf with white water all around you might enhance your ride and even give you the opportunity to pull off a couple more moves before you turn and head back out to sea.

White water waves have so many great features

Shallow water close to the shore. You're close to the beach and therefore relatively safe. There's no need to have a perfect roll; wipe out and swim in this zone and you'll be back in your kayak in next to no time.

A huge range of size and power. You can select the power and size of the white water wave to match your mood. Feeling brave, then paddle out to where the white water waves are at their biggest, feeling timid then stay close to the beach and develop your skills just as well.

Surrounded by friends. You'll be away from the experts and the egos. The soup can be a much friendlier place than the line-up. Everyone surfing white water waves is learning so messing up here is expected!

Common sense replaces surf etiquette. Because the wave has broken you can forget about the rule of one person per wave. As long as you keep a safe distance apart there can be any number of surfers enjoying the same ride. For you this means less waiting around and more time surfing.

"The soup can be a much friendlier place than the line-up."

"just like the green wave

a white water wave also

has a sloping face."

How green waves and white water waves are related

To me it sounds like a good place to practise but you might be wondering how a manoeuvre on a white water wave has anything in common with surfing a green wave; surely the properties of these waves are completely different?

At first glance you might think so. The green wave is smooth and sloping whereas the white water wave is turbulent and shaped like a fist punching its way to the beach. Get yourself side on to the surf and have another look and you'll see, much to your amazement, that just like the green wave a white water wave also has a sloping face. Sure it might have the profile of a clenched fist as the green wave explosively breaks and forms the white water wave but almost immediately afterwards the profile changes into a sloping wedge. And one slope is very similar to another when you're working on your moves.

Manoeuvres using white water waves

We've already seen in the last chapter how white water waves are ideal for developing core stability and edge awareness but they are also ideal for practising a whole string of more advanced manoeuvres. Not only that but there are some manoeuvres (popouts and cartwheels) that have their home in the white water. There are even paddle out strategies that are specific to this zone.

The arse and sweep paddle-out method

Do you ever get really sick of paddling out through line after line of white water? Although each wave is shaped like a wedge the leading edge is naturally turbulent. If you just paddle straight at it the nose of your kayak will bury into this turbulent mass of water and you'll get hit in the guts with the full force of the wave. Each time this happens you get pushed back to shore and end up wasting valuable energy on your paddle out.

If only you could just skim over the approaching waves, without any push back at all. The arse and sweep method allows you to do just that. Paddle fast towards the approaching wave at an angle of about 45°. As you're about to hit the leading edge of the wave lean back, show the wave your arse and sweep hard on your beachward side. Time this right and you'll skim right up and over the white water without so much as a drop of water coming over the deck of your boat.

This method works because by turning your boat to 45° you increase the effect of its rocker. By leaning back you lighten the nose and actually cause the front of your kayak to rise slightly out of the water, ensuring that the nose will ride over the approaching turbulent edge of the wave. By showing your arse to the wave you raise the seaward edge of your kayak and so create a seaward skimming hull, allowing water to pass under you with little resistance. The beachward sweep powers you up and over the white water slope and at the same time straightens you up, ensuring that you don't get caught side on. Finally return to a forward leaning body position as you're skimming up the wave as this ensures that the kayak is well trimmed and won't get dragged back down the face.

When you perfect this approach you'll be amazed at the size of the white water slope you can skim over, but don't try it on a just-broken wave as the white water slope won't have settled into place and you'll get hammered!

"Time this right and you'll skim right up and over

the white water without so much as a drop of water

coming over the deck of your boat."

The paddle-out take off

Performing a paddle-out take-off in white water waves is relatively easy. Get your technique sorted here and you'll then be able to adapt it to the more critical peeling power pocket zone.

Start from the shore and paddle out over a couple of waves. When you see the next powerful white water wave approaching carry on paddling towards it at about 45°. Before the wave hits the front of your kayak, pre-rotate your head, neck and shoulders to look back towards the beach.

Now, as the wave hits the nose of your boat, pull your lower body around to face the same direction as your upper body and hey presto! you'll be surfing back towards the shore.

The power of the wave and good pre-rotation of your upper body will provide all the force required to turn your legs and your kayak back towards the shore. A sweep stroke on the seaward side of your boat or a mid boat pivot (a bit like a pry stroke in line with your hips) on the beachward side will sharpen and speed up the turn.

As the front end of your kayak gets pushed sharply around ensure that you hold a skimming edge by means of a slight but firm raising of your boat's beachward edge. With your hull held in this skimming edge position you'll minimise any resistance to this turn.

As you approach your chosen wave sit upright maintaining good functional stability. Just before you hit the wave rotate your head and shoulders to face back to the shore.

At the moment of impact it's the pulling around of your legs that helps to power the turn. Your forward leaning body position keeps you stable and stops the tail of your kayak from snagging half way through the turn. Leaning forwards also creates good trim, so maximising your chances of continuing your ride down the white water slope of the wave.

Bottom turns

White water waves are an excellent place to practise and perfect your bottom turns. They've all the features you need: a slope to fall down; calm unbroken water at their base in which your kayak can carve around the turn; and an easy way to measure your success.

Speed, space and timing are the critical components for the bottom turn. Consider how your speed varies as you drop down the face of a wave. You accelerate from a slow start to a maximum speed somewhere near the bottom of the face. However if you continue to run out in front of the wave you'll soon lose this speed and come to a grinding halt. When you practise bottom turns on white water waves you'll start to feel how your speed changes as you drop down the slope and you'll learn that good timing will give you the speed and space required for a good turn.

Turn too early when you've little speed and with no space in which to turn and you'll end up side on to the wave, bongo sliding to the beach. Turn too late and although you'll have plenty of space out in front of the wave you'll have lost all your speed. Your turn may start OK but it'll die before you're half way around. The wave will eventually catch up and once again you'll be bongo sliding to the beach.

Time your bottom turn for when you're travelling at maximum speed and you'll have both the speed and the space out in front of the wave to carve your boat in a full arc so that it ends up facing back towards the very wave you've just descended. A positive end to this manoeuvre, on a white water wave would be when the nose of your kayak comes back into contact with the wave before the rest of the kayak. You're then in a position to punch back through the wave and end your ride.

So with your focus firmly on the timing of this manoeuvre, catch a nice powerful white water wave, accelerate down its slope, keeping your body leaning forwards to maximise your trim. Reach out to the inside of your planned turn with your paddle creating a skimming outrigger. This helps to initiate the turn and also keeps your body out of the water as you lean into the turn. Edge your boat hard on its inside rail, let your body lean out and keep your shoulders and head steady, focusing on the end of the turn.

Remember that bottom turns are high speed, long, drawn out, carving turns that need a hard inside edge cutting deep into the water throughout the turn. Lose that edge and your kayak will spin out. You might still end up facing out to sea but you'll have lost all your speed and as the wave catches you up expect to be held in its grip rather than being able to punch through it to escape.

"Remember that bottom turns are high speed, long, drawn out, carving turns that need a hard inside edge cutting deep into the water throughout the turn."

"As the turbulent white water wave hits the nose of your kayak encourage it to turn back towards the shore by lessening your edge and rotating your body"

180° turns

These are a sequence of turns that form the basis of the cutback turn used on a green peeling wave. 180° turns or white water cutbacks link the high speed carving bottom turn with a low speed pivot and skim top turn. Essentially take the bottom turn (discussed previously) and follow it with the procedure for a paddle-out take-off (also discussed previously).

Imagine catching a white water wave and dropping down its slope. As you reach your maximum speed at the base of the slope, carve a bottom turn off to your right-hand side. As your kayak carves around this turn you'll be facing back towards your wave at something like 45°. As the turbulent white water wave hits the nose of your kayak encourage it to turn back towards the shore by lessening your edge and rotating your body. A sweep or beachward pivot stroke will sharpen this turn. If your timing is good then you'll once again start to fall back down the slope of the wave.

You're now essentially back at the start of your ride, falling down the slope about to carve another bottom turn. However this time turn left instead of right. Carry on riding the wave with a sequence of right bottom turn, crash back into the white water and top turn, drop down the wave, left bottom turn, crash back into the white water and top turn, drop down the wave, right bottom turn and so on. You'll start to develop progressively better positioning for the turns in this sequence giving you an improved feel for the characteristics of the wave itself.

Popouts, pirouettes and cartwheels

The traditional end-moves of surf kayaking, all involving slicing your kayak's nose well and truly into the still water in front of the wave, allowing it to stall and upend both you and your kayak.

It's the approach to these moves that has changed most in recent years. When surf kayaking first came into existence popouts were performed in long high volume craft falling down the biggest and steepest of waves. Nowadays the same result can be achieved in a much more controlled way by essentially performing a skim and pivot top turn on a white water wave and allowing the beachward edge to catch as the turn develops.

Imagine the sequence of moves described previously for the 180° turns. As the sequence of bottom turn followed by top turn continues, start to plan for a popout. As you crash back into the white water wave and initiate your next low speed pivot and skim top turn, lean heavily on your beachward pivot stroke and start to let the nose of your kayak skim around.

If facing directly to the shore represents 12 o'clock then in this example we're aiming to let our kayak's nose skim around anticlockwise to reach 2 o'clock. At this point, still leaning heavily on your beachward pivot stroke, drop your beachward knee, increase your forward leaning body position and allow the front beachward edge of your kayak to catch in the water. Hold this position as your rotation

"Perform a skim and pivot top turn on a white water wave and allow the beachward edge to catch as the turn develops."

brings you around to 12 o'clock with the nose of your kayak slicing deeper into the water. You and your boat have now stalled and are balanced in an up ended position.

For the popout simply push down on your feet and lean back in a standing up position, and let the trapped buoyancy of your kayak pop you back up. For the pirouette stand up again but this time push forwards on your beachward pivot stroke (which should still be in the water), look over your shoulder and you should pop up and spin around at the same time, increasing your chances of landing upright and facing out to sea.

For the cartwheel, initially engage the nose of your kayak a little later so that your rotation through the top turn brings you past 12 o'clock. You're now stalled in your up-ended kayak and facing at an angle across the wave rather than straight to the shore. Keep leaning forwards whilst rotating your body in order to whip the tail of your kayak down into the water, reach across your body with your beachward paddle blade, lean back and push the nose of your kayak through the air towards the shore.

The best thing about practising these moves in white water waves is that if you fail to engage the nose of your kayak in the water then you can just carry on with your fall down the wave, bottom turn and then have another go as you crash once again back into the wave.

Developing judgement

And as a bonus all that time you're surfing in the white water zone you'll be gaining vital experience. Without even knowing it your ability to read the wave will be improving. Fairly soon you'll be able to select certain features within the body of the wave; you might benefit from a surge of power or a weak spot may enable you to pull off the wave and finish your ride.

Initially haphazard events will start to follow a pattern and you'll start to recognise this pattern and relate it back to your actions and the environment. You'll start to plan ahead looking for features or planning moves before you need them.

Your decision making and judgement, in terms of paddling out and the waves that you select to ride, will become refined. You'll start to see details you've never noticed before, a slight change in wind direction, a small change in current, the effect of a change in posture.

Kenny King selecting just the

right moment to hit the lip

"Spending time in this zone develops your skills and judgement and will make you a much more refined and safer surfer when you next venture out to surf the green waves."

Summary

Making the most of the white water environment makes a great deal of sense. Spending time in this zone develops your skills and judgement and will make you a much more refined and safer surfer when you next venture out to surf the green waves. In addition to the white water zone being an excellent practice ground for moves such as the paddle-out take-off and the bottom turn, it's also the home of many specific manoeuvres including the arse and sweep method for paddling out, 180° turns, the popout, pirouette and cartwheel.

* In the white water zone you're close to the beach and so in a relatively safe area. You can select the power and size of the wave to match your mood.

* Common sense takes priority over surf etiquette. As long as you keep a safe distance apart there can be any number of surfers enjoying the same ride.

* White water waves might have the profile of a clenched fist at the moment they are formed but almost immediately their profile changes into a sloping wedge.

* Perfect the arse and sweep method of paddling out over white water waves in order to save energy and time.

* A paddle-out take-off in white water waves is a great way to perfect pre-rotation and to isolate the skills required for a pivot and skim top turn.

* White water waves are an excellent place to practise and perfect your bottom turns.

* 180° turns or white water cutbacks link high speed carving bottom turns with low speed pivot and skim top turns.

* Popouts, pirouettes and cartwheels performed on the white water wave are the traditional end-moves of surf kayaking.

* All that time you're surfing in the white water zone you'll be gaining vital experience and developing good judgement.

BECOMING AN EXPERT

Introduction

I remember reading a book about acquiring skills and knowledge and the difference between being an expert and a novice. The book used two chess players to explain the differences but it could so easily have used two surfers! When looking at the chess board the novice sees the chess pieces as they are, the moves he makes are simple isolated events. The expert chess player sees not just the chess pieces but the whole development of the game, her moves will be the complex result of the interaction of her own strategy and that of her opponent.

Now consider two surfers stood on the cliff top looking out at the break. Ask the novice what he sees and the answer will be limited to perhaps a guess at the size of the waves, a comment about the general weather and the number of surfers already in the water. Ask the expert and their reply will be detailed and specific. They'll see the peaks, the rips, currents, swell direction, effects of the wind and local geography, set characteristics, character of the wave and the quality of the other surfers. They will evaluate how all of this will be affected as the tide and weather changes in the next couple of hours. But why does an enthusiastic surfer end up with such an expert eye? The answer is simply because it matters! It matters not just in terms of safety but also in terms of the quality of their surfing experience.

"But why does an enthusiastic surfer end up with such an expert eye? The answer is simply because it matters! It matters not just in terms of safety but also in terms of the quality of their surfing experience."

"An expert would see rips and channels as
an easy way of getting out through the surf. "

What the expert sees from the shore

Rips and channels. Created by deep gullies or trenches where water is generally flowing back out to sea. An expert would see rips and channels as an easy way of getting out through the surf. Identified by the lack of breaking surf, or an area where the surf is backing off. When the surf is producing lots of white water waves the rips and channels are often identified as areas that remain blue whilst the water to either side is left dappled by the passing waves. Because the water in a rip is moving in a different direction to the nearby stationary water it can often be identified as having a different surface appearance. It might catch more wind and so appear choppy or be carrying debris and foam back out to sea.

Currents. Often associated with headlands where tidal currents are compressed to form a faster flow or race. The strength of a tidal current and the effect it has on a surfer depends on large scale coastal geography, local features and the state of the tide. Identified in the same way as rips by having a different surface appearance to neighbouring water or carrying a line of debris or foam. Paddlers will experience the worst tidal currents when surfing in the following conditions:

* off a coastline associated with off-shore islands or deep sea channels;
* at a break found at the end of a headland;
* during spring tides; and
* at a time half way through the tidal range.

Swell direction. Look beyond the break at the lines of swell travelling across the ocean. Although they'll straighten up as they approach the shore they will still exhibit features linked to the direction from which they originated. Subtle changes in swell direction can have enormous effects on the quality of the breaking wave. At a well known point break not far from where I live a southerly swell will create a slow peeling wave, a south-westerly swell creates a fast hollow peeling wave whereas a north-westerly swell just closes the wave out. Weather information and expert observation will give you clues as to the origin of the swell and past experiences will help you to predict what effect this may have.

The effect of the wind. On-shore, off-shore and cross-shore winds will have huge effects on the quality of the breaking wave (see terminology section). Not only the direction but the strength of the wind needs to be taken into consideration. White horses out to sea are a sure sign of a strong wind and one that may affect a paddler's ability to control their position in the surf. Surfers in the water will provide additional clues. If they are constantly having to paddle just to stay in position then so will you if you decide to join them. Strong off-shore winds can be very dangerous. In addition, they can flatten out the swell and will seriously hamper catching a wave.

The effect of local geography. Find a break that's protected by high cliffs and the negative effects of a strong off-shore wind will be vastly reduced. In a similar way cross-shore winds can be reduced by a conveniently situated headland. Cliffs and valleys near the shore can, however, have stranger effects on the wind. High cliffs can cause sudden down drafts that may take paddlers completely by surprise and valleys will often redirect the wind to follow their path, resulting in an off-shore wind when a cross-shore was expected.

Set characteristics. The perfect situation for all surfers would be for a wave to come along whenever you wanted one, followed by a lull that allowed you to paddle back out without so much as getting your hair wet. Such a situation is not beyond reality, especially if you have a well defined set of waves arriving at the shore at regular intervals. Spend time watching the pattern of sets arriving at the break. Try to get an idea of how many waves are in each set and the time between sets. With a keen eye backed up by experience in the water you'll even be able to identify the largest wave in a set. All of this information will make for an easier and less frustrating surfing experience.

Where is the peak? The peak, line-up or take-off zone is never in a completely fixed position (see terminology section and the next chapter) due to the ever changing size of waves and the steady movement of the tide. However there are some useful clues that can help you to identify it. Look for the dappled water, that is the white water left on the surface after a broken wave has passed. The position of the outer edge of this dappled region shows you where the wave starts to break and the shape of this region shows you how the wave breaks. You can use the edge of the dappled zone once you're afloat to guide you out to the peak. Once there, line up objects back on the shore to form a transit. This is a technique I use all the time, especially if I'm fighting a current or crosswind and need to be accurately positioned for a good take-off.

Quality and character of the breaking waves. The same dappled water that indicates the position of the peak can be extremely useful in diagnosing the way in which the waves are breaking. If the zone of dappled water has a diagonal edge it's a good sign indicating a peeling wave whereas a straight rear edge, parallel to the shore, is a bad sign indicating a close out wave. If the dappled water finishes before the shore then you'll know that the waves here will be backing off as they disappear into a deep trench or gully. Other signs in the water include boils, where water plunging deep from a breaking wave is violently redirected up to the surface, a sure indication of a shallow bank or isolated submerged rocks. When sand is sucked to the surface by a breaking wave you can be sure that the wave is breaking with considerable power. This could be exactly what you're after or a signal to surf elsewhere. Remember large waves that rear up and almost break further out to sea will be breaking for real as the tide drops. Conversely, smaller waves that have a better breaking shape than the set waves are an indication of how the set waves will break as the tide comes in.

Quality and quantity of other surfers. Although a very individual pursuit we hardly ever surf alone. On a sandy beach break there can be surfers spread across the whole bay, where as at a point or reef break surfers may be gathered in a very tight area. Whatever the situation, reading the ability and characteristics of these surfers will help in choosing where you want to surf.

When it's busy the most popular and easy to get to breaks fill up first. If the set waves are in limited supply then frustration becomes the overwhelming emotion, tempers flair, chances are taken and etiquette gets thrown out of the window. These are the conditions that lead to surf rage. I'd be back in the car looking for a quieter break because, even if the quality of the waves is slightly worse elsewhere, the quality of the experience is bound to be so much better.

Look out for the surfers who are getting the best of the waves. These are the guys who are in the right place at the right time and they're a good example to follow. However, my advice before paddling straight out and joining the pro's is to work through a mini-apprenticeship. Catch a couple of smaller waves, show the pack what you can do and as you join the line-up be patient and take your turn. This will earn you more respect than just barging in. Finally always keep an eye out for the learners. They're often in the white water zone, but not always. These surfers might not know all the road rules and could be a danger to you.

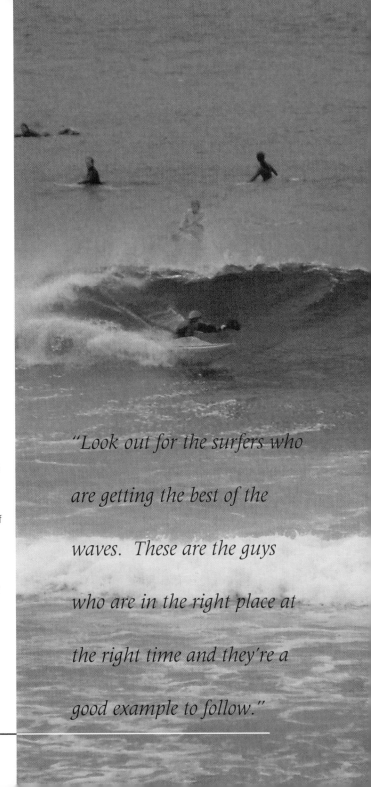

"Look out for the surfers who are getting the best of the waves. These are the guys who are in the right place at the right time and they're a good example to follow."

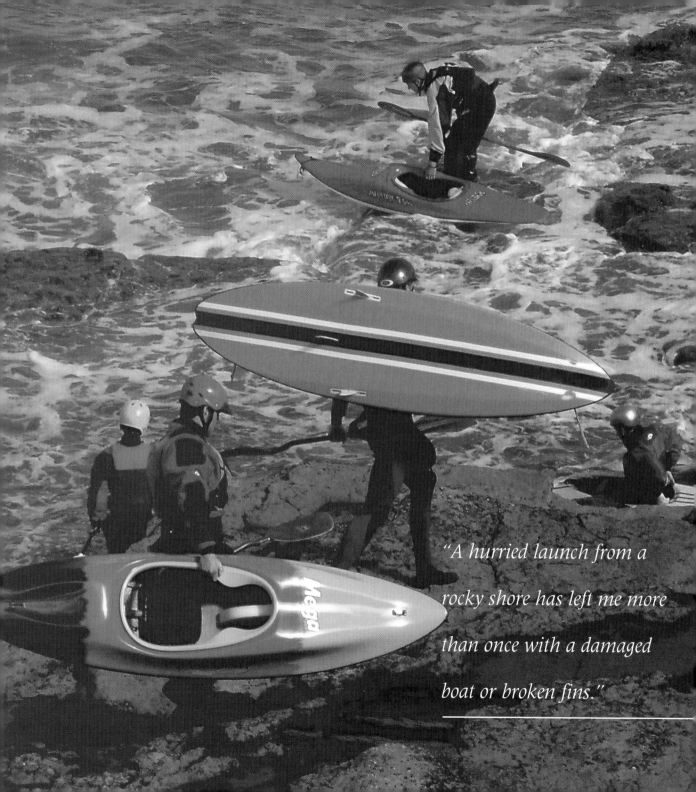

"A hurried launch from a rocky shore has left me more than once with a damaged boat or broken fins."

Launching

Where to launch is probably the surf kayaker's biggest problem, especially in a high performance (finned) surf kayak. How frustrating to have identified a fantastic break only to then realise that there's no way into the water without wrecking your boat. Haste won't help, as I've often found out to my cost. A hurried launch from a rocky shore has left me more than once with a damaged boat or broken fins.

Launching from a soft sandy beach sounds ideal but even here the shape of the beach, the movement of the tide and the surging nature of the surf can make life difficult. If you've ever got the chance to launch into a sheltered, still, channel of water leading into the surf then take it. This will always be a lot less traumatic and tiresome than launching directly into the swell. If a direct launch is your only option then my advice is to spend some time watching the waves, wait for a lull and launch close to the waters edge but don't be totally afloat. Practise getting in, doing up your straps and getting your spraydeck on as quickly as possible. A fast entry into your kayak means less chance of being caught, filled up and spun around by a surging wave and having to start all over again.

Launching from rocky shores can be even more difficult. Without fins there's always the possibility of launching directly from the rocks. Just choose your rock wisely, avoid abrasive shells, keep an eye on the swell, get into your kayak at the speed of light and time your entry to perfection. By re-locating you may be able to find a much more suitable launch site with less swell and a softer surface from which to launch. The mounds of kelp at Easkey, Western Ireland made for a very easy launch for competitors at a recent World Championships. Expecting a problem with launching some paddlers had arrived with their very own launching pads and trolleys, great ideas especially if you regularly launch from a rocky shore or from concrete slipways.

Paddling out

I was once at a surf symposium held at Widemouth Bay in North Cornwall. Down the beach a little way from me was a very senior coach by the name of Nigel Robinson who was advising two inexperienced paddlers how to get out through the breaking waves. He briefed them on the need for good timing and for caution, essential if they were to get beyond the impact zone where wave after wave was exploding in front of them. I'd left the beach shortly after this group and hadn't heard Nigel's briefing so just paddled out as normal. I slowly approached the impact zone and then got really mad! With Motorhead's 'Ace of Spades' playing in my head I charged right into the mouth of the next breaking monster; it ate me, gave me a good thrashing and spat me out. I rolled up and charged right into the mouth of another monster but this time I managed to punch right through the back of the wave to emerge upright and in clear water. I still had to sprint to get over the next rearing wave but then I was out.

A few minutes later I was joined by a laughing Nigel and his two students. They'd been patient and cautious and when there'd been a lull between waves had paddled out with relative ease. So who was right? Well, we all made it out beyond the break but I was the one that had got hammered! Selecting the right paddling out strategy on a given day can make a huge difference. It's not a case of being tough or being timid but of choosing and blending a range of techniques, and using the environment to your advantage.

Use whatever the environment gives you: it might be a rip current, a channel, a gap between sets, a harbour wall, the shelter from a headland or breakwater. You might not need this extra help the first time you paddle out but you sure as hell will after your 20th wave. Use this natural help from the start and stay fresher longer. When you're paddling out through the breaking surf constantly adjust your line to make the most of unbroken or low energy parts of the incoming waves. At the end of a ride don't just turn around and head straight back out the way you surfed in. Apart from bad etiquette you'll use up far more energy crashing through powerful surf than if you first paddled away from the breaking waves and circled back out to the peak.

If you do have to get over or through incoming breaking waves then you've a handful of options to choose from. Faced with a rearing monster about to break on my head my course of action has ranged from the daring charge-and-punch-through to a desperate last minute roll or turning and running with the wave.

"Selecting the right paddling

out strategy on a given day

can make a huge difference."

Choosing the best line for paddling out avoids having to struggle through white water.

Charge and punch through

The best practitioner I know of the charge and punch through method is English surfer Gary Adcock. His approach to the ever rearing wave face is aggressive and extremely well timed. As the wave hollows out, Gary thrusts the nose of his kayak into the hollow face of the wave with his body position so far forwards his face is almost touching the deck. As he punches through the wave face everything is streamlined: boat, body and paddles. Then as he emerges out the back of the wave a rapid sequence of paddle strokes pulls him clear of the wave's suck-back.

Rolling

If you're too late to punch through then rolling may be a good option. It's certainly better than having the full force of a wave land on your head or in your lap, which is likely to pop your spray deck. However, rolling doesn't always enhance your chances of getting beyond the break. Get it wrong and you'll be pushed back towards the shore, sometimes caught in the turbulent heart of the wave surfing upside down until either the wave releases you or you bail out.

I've found the most positive way of rolling through the surf is to paddle hard at the incoming wave, turn slightly just before contact then roll away from the wave. This action will ensure that the natural turbulence of the wave will assist rather than hinder your rolling action. Once under the water keep your paddles in close, arms bent and lean forwards. If you do get taken by the wave the last thing you want is to have your shoulders dislocated or your back hyper extended. Then wait, it's important not to try and roll up too soon as you'll be pulling your paddle against aerated water, literally pulling against thin air. Wait until everything goes calm and then your roll will be as easy as doing it in a swimming pool.

"As he punches through the wave everything is streamlined: boat, body and paddles."

Turn and run

Turning and running with the wave is an interesting paddle out option. For starters you're not exactly paddling out! But there are situations when it may well be the best immediate option available. I've certainly turned and run with a wave rather than get trashed by yet another avalanche of white water.

There comes a point when you can't keep holding your breath for yet another extended roll and you simply know that no matter what you do this incoming wave is going to pulverise you. Physically and mentally you need a time-out. So rather than swim or get washed in why not turn and run with the wave. Pick up as much speed as you can, lean well back and get ready to be hit by a truck. You'll have no real control for the first couple of seconds, just concentrate on not catching an edge. If you're still upright then you'll be able to ride the white water wave in and take that time-out. When you're physically and mentally recovered, reassess your paddle out strategy and have another go.

"Pick up as much speed as you can, lean well back and get ready to be hit by a truck."

Summary

You can't develop an expert's eye overnight but you don't need to take years to do it either. There's no better motivation than being interested and if you're really interested in this sport then you'll start to see the details and learn the techniques very quickly. Try to be as independent as you can, make your own plans and take your own decisions. You'll make mistakes but with reflection you'll understand why and you'll learn. The more you can see, the more techniques you have at your disposal, the better your chances of having a safe, high quality surfing experience.

✴ An expert view of the surfing environment matters not just in terms of safety but also in terms of the quality of the experience.

✴ A novice may well see the main features but an expert sees the details that will affect the quality of the surfing experience.

✴ Launching is probably the surf kayaker's biggest problem. A fast entry into your kayak means less chance of being caught, filled up and spun around by a surging wave and having to start all over again.

✴ Paddling out is about choosing and blending a range of techniques and using the environment to your advantage.

"There's no better motivation than being interested and if you're really interested in this sport then you'll start to see the details and learn the techniques very quickly."

THE TAKE-OFF

Introduction

"All over in less than a second, yet the way you catch the wave is probably the most important part of the ride."

All over in less than a second, yet the way you catch the wave is probably the most important part of the ride. Get it wrong and your ride is over before you even start; get it right and you're in the perfect part of the wave with speed and as much room to play with as you wish. Such an important and complex skill and yet so often overlooked.

So what's so complex about the take-off? Well to start with it's not as simple as it seems. Watch an expert surfer and it appears that they just paddle a couple of strokes towards the beach and hey presto! they're on the wave. This apparent simplicity masks a great many variables and options. What's really just happened is the result of a sound assessment, good judgement, correct positioning and a split second decision that will match the take-off angle to the features of the wave.

A sound assessment

It all started back on the beach when you were assessing the conditions. You'll have noted the size of the swell and the way it breaks. You'll have identified the zone where the wave begins to break and the frequency of the sets. You'll have taken into account the effects of the wind and currents and you may even have had the opportunity to watch a few other surfers in the water as they attempt to ride that same wave. You'll have planned your route out to the line-up and identified features that will help you to know when you're there. And if you haven't, well, your chances of even getting close to a good take-off are reduced to pure luck!

Positioning in and around the take-off zone

Being an intelligent surfer you find yourself paddling out through the surf towards the spot where you're hoping to catch your waves. Being particularly clever you've timed your paddle out to coincide with a lull in the sets. You have then zeroed in on your chosen take-off zone by using clues in the water (dappled water left by the last set) and by lining up features back on the shore.

Waiting in the take-off zone ought to be your chance to rest and relax. It's a time and place to chill out, to chat to your friends and reflect on all that is right with the world. But don't relax too much. You're in a dynamic environment and if you're caught out of position when the next set thunders through then you can kiss goodbye to a good ride.

The problem with being well positioned in the take-off zone is movement. You'll be constantly moved about by both wind and currents and the take-off zone is continually being repositioned by the size of the breaking waves and the state of the tide. You've got to keep your eyes and ears open. If the sets are few and far between then move back towards the shore and pick off some smaller waves, but stay alert. When someone in the group shouts "outside", don't hang around, it's a signal that a larger than normal wave is on the way. With an experienced eye you'll get to recognise how the horizon changes when a big wave is approaching. The crest of a large approaching swell will actually become the horizon line; spot this early enough and you'll have time to paddle further out and reposition to catch this wave.

Getting into position for the best take-off is not just about moving closer in to shore or further out to sea. For any given wave, on any given day there will be an ideal take-off spot - hard to tell exactly where this will be but nevertheless it's there. You may decide to position yourself as near as possible to this imaginary spot or you may decide for very good reasons to wait at some distance and direction from this point.

"With an experienced eye you'll get to recognise how the horizon changes when a big wave is approaching."

One surfer catches a wave but what are the other three looking at?

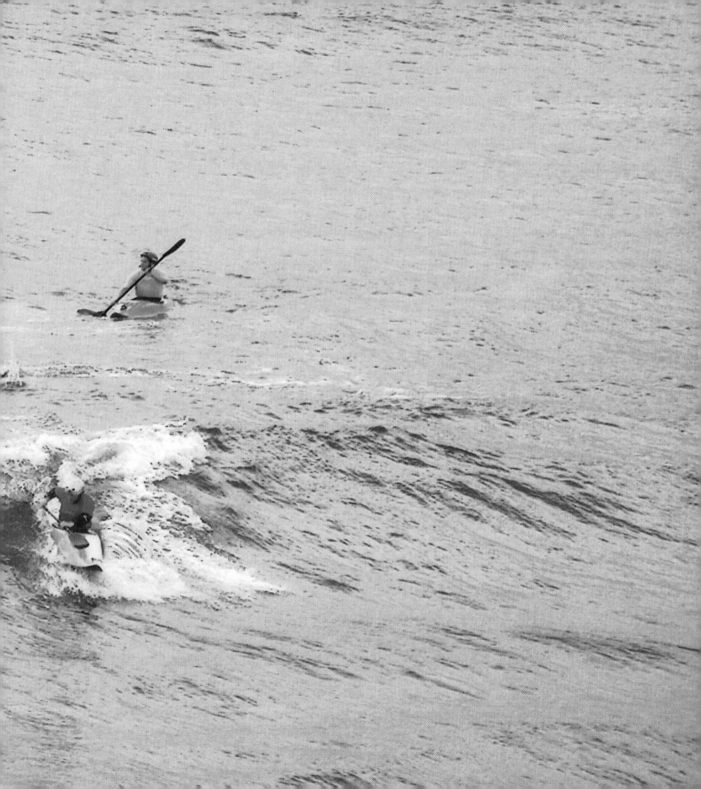

Waiting positions relative to the ideal take-off spot

Further out to sea. A safe place to wait where you can relax. You might want a bit of a rest or have decided that it's time to let some of the other surfers have a wave. If you're still actively looking to catch a wave then, with good timing, you can gradually pick up speed as you approach the take-off zone and catch the wave with little additional effort. However, approaching the take-off zone with the wave directly behind you means that it's difficult to read the way the wave will break and it's therefore easy to be out of position.

Closer towards the shore. Always at risk of being caught inside and so for some types of break this is just too dangerous a place to wait. However, on sandy beach breaks, waiting slightly further in than the other surfers often means that you're in a good position to pick off some of the nicer, smaller waves. In the long run you'll catch more waves. You'll need to stay alert and reposition yourself quickly when the set waves approach and accept that every now and again you'll get caught by a breaking wave. Most of the time you'll be facing out to sea, easily able to read the approaching wave and at the same time move into position to catch it. Don't forget to recheck your position in relation to shore in case you've drifted towards danger.

Deep. Waiting deep simply means that for a right hand peeling wave you're waiting deep to the left of the optimum take-off spot or for a left hander you're waiting deep to the right. This is where the brave surfer waits! Brave because you're waiting in a position where the repercussions of getting it wrong are at their worst. Where if you're even just a little too deep when you try and catch the wave you'll be eaten by the full force of a crashing lip and obliterated. So why even think of waiting deep? Quite simply because waiting deep gives you right of way. As a swell approaches you can pick up speed as you move towards the take-off spot. Other surfers will be repositioning towards that same take-off spot but you'll have speed in the right direction and the inside line and therefore you'll have right of way over all of them. Approaching the take-off spot from a deep position requires commitment and good judgement but you'll be rewarded with an early adrenaline rush and high speed take-offs.

Out to the side. This is the opposite of waiting deep. You're out in line with the take-off spot but off to the side so that if you tried to catch the wave from

"approaching the take-off zone with the wave directly behind you means that it's difficult to read the way the wave will break and it's therefore easy to be out of position."

Two paddlers waiting in the channel look on as a third paddler works hard to reach the take-off spot.

this position you'd find that the wave would still be a shallow sloping swell. Waiting out to this side, especially on a point break or reef break, is just as safe, if not safer, than waiting further out to sea with the massive advantage that you can look across from your position and actually see where the approaching wave will break. On big days when you're surfing with a bunch of friends this is a great place to wait - you can watch the approaching swell and decide whether or not to paddle across to the take-off spot. If you're going for the wave then, with the wave in view, you can angle your approach so you're in the perfect position at just the right moment to achieve the perfect take-off. If there's lots of surfers in the water then consistently approaching the take-off spot from this angle could lead to frustration. You'll find that you'll often have to give way to the surfer who has approached the take-off spot from a deeper position. It's best for you to reposition rather than let your frustration turn into blatant drop-ins.

Hitting the take-off spot, acceleration and speed

Ok we're almost there: you've assessed all the environmental variables, you've identified the take-off zone, approached the take-off spot aaaaaaaaand you're off...well not quite. You see the thing is that after all this great preparation we can still mess it up. But surely there's nothing left to get wrong, is there? Well just a couple of things.

Your speed at the moment of take-off is critical. We've talked about approaching the take-off spot and this obviously involves your kayak travelling at some sort of speed. This approach-speed is more to do with getting to the right spot at the right time; it's not yet about catching the wave.

When I think about being caught by a fast moving wave I picture one of those Charlie Chaplin slapstick comedies where he and a mate are slowly rolling along a railroad on a hand pumped cart when suddenly a steam train comes into view behind them. However fast they pump the cart the train is going to catch them. If they carry on pumping slowly the train will smash right into them and knock them and the cart flying. However if they pump that cart with all their might, accelerating the cart faster and faster, then as the train catches them there will be a much smoother contact.

To catch a wave smoothly you've got to be travelling as fast as Charlie Chaplin - really fast - the sort of fast that comes from 100% maximum paddling effort. Maximum effort, but unlike Charlie you shouldn't have to sustain this maximum effort for long. In fact if you've manoeuvred into the take-off spot at exactly the right moment then most of the effort required to get you to take-off speed will come from the wave itself.

What you're aiming for is not just maximum speed but maximum acceleration. Short paddles will help to keep your powerful short strokes efficient. Good forward body position and a correctly positioned seat in your kayak will give you optimum trim. A lighter kayak will accelerate faster than a heavier one and a longer, less rockered kayak will have less drag than a shorter highly rockered one. But above all else it's the combination of take-off position and powerful paddling that will optimise your take-off.

Hit the take-off spot at exactly the right moment and you can accelerate to take-off speed in less than two powerful strokes. If you are regularly using ten or more powerful strokes to catch a wave then you're in the wrong position. If you can't catch a wave or get obliterated by every wave you do catch then it's a combination of poor positioning and lack of power. Paddle at a pace that meets your requirements. By all means paddle slowly when you're moving into position but turn on your afterburner when you're about to catch that wave.

"paddle slowly when you're moving into

position but turn on your afterburner

when you're about to catch that wave."

"Paddle diagonally towards the power pocket then bounce off the white water for a cut back."

Angle down the face

As the wave moves under you and you pick up speed you've a split second to adjust the line you plan to follow. As you take-off on the wave your kayak is in transition between the features of a displacement hull and that of a planing hull. You're at the top of the wave face, on the very verge of breaking free from the suction of the surrounding water. Your boat is almost unstuck and yet you're still at a speed where you can control your direction with a paddle stroke. So make the most of it. Your last stroke can have a profound effect on what happens next.

Try to look ahead, picture how the wave is going to break and then try to match where you want to be with the most appropriate take-off angle. It's hard to get right, especially at a new break on the very first wave. It's hard to get right because so often we develop our own style of take-off, with an angle that matches the waves at our local break. Then when we go somewhere new we're caught out by a wave that's breaking differently and at a different speed. We've got plenty of options and there's always one that will fit.

Straight down the face. The best angle for acceleration. A good choice on slow breaking waves or steep waves with a slow peeling speed. Dropping vertically down the face is usually followed by a high speed carving turn (bottom turn) that will redirect your speed across the wave face. Watch out for hollow fast peeling waves as this take-off angle and bottom turn combination will often end up with you inside the tube, whether you want to be there or not!

Diagonally down the face. After you've set this angle with your last paddle stroke you'll have to engage the seaward edge of your kayak into the wave face in order to hold your line. A good choice on a very fast peeling wave, as not only will you accelerate down the wave but you'll also be running away from the fast approaching power pocket which otherwise threatens to engulf you.

Diagonally towards the power pocket. If you're out to the side of the wave but still have the chance to catch it then this is a useful direction for your take-off. It's going to require a longer period of sustained paddling but as you catch the shallow swell, angle your take-off diagonally towards the oncoming power pocket. As you get closer you'll accelerate into the pocket where you can either bounce off the white water for a cut back or simply carve around in the pocket to face back the way you've come.

Regain. A regain is where you've caught a wave and either due to a miscalculation or competition in the water you find that you're the wrong side of the peeling lip. In some cases (mainly beach breaks) you could just decide to surf the other way across the wave face but in other situations there's only one safe direction in which to go. The trick here is to drop down and around the breaking lip and regain the power pocket on the other side. If you can do this in one flowing move then you'll still have right of way. However if the regain is protracted or involves additional paddling then don't expect anyone to give up the wave.

Summary

So there you have it. The humble take-off: just a simple matter of assessing conditions, identifying the take-off zone, good positioning, acceleration and angle. You're not going to get it right first time or indeed every time. The more often you get your take-off right the more waves you'll catch and the more frequently you'll be in the best position to maximise your ride.

* Get your take-off wrong and your ride is over before you even start; get it right and you're in the perfect part of the wave with speed and room to play with.

* Without a sound assessment of conditions your chances of even getting close to a good take-off are reduced to pure luck!

* Use clues in the water (dappled water left by the last set) and line up features back on the shore to help identify the take-off zone.

* Carefully consider where you wait for the next wave.

* Hit the take-off spot at exactly the right moment and you can accelerate to take-off speed in less than two powerful strokes.

* As you're taking off try to look ahead, picture how the wave is going to break and then try to match where you want to be with the most appropriate take- off angle.

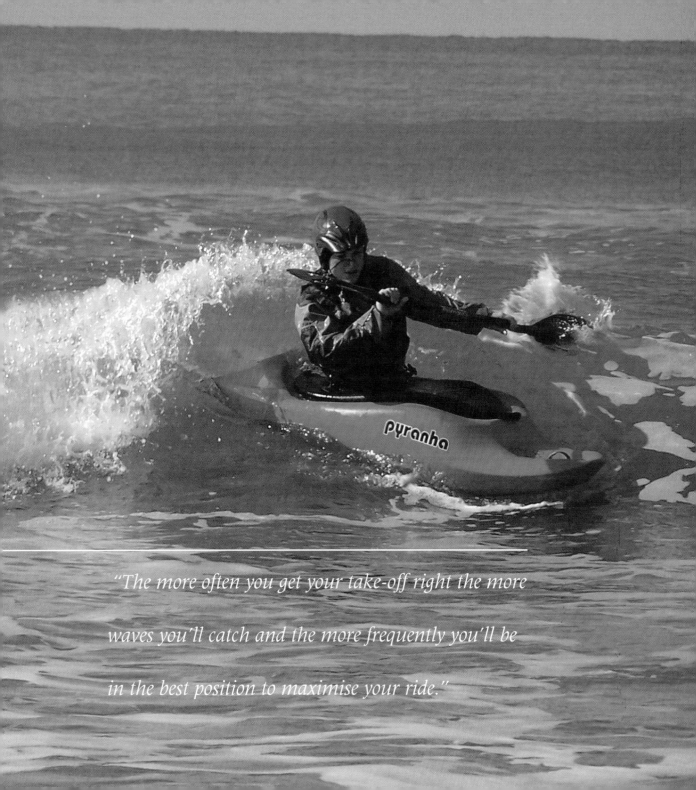

"The more often you get your take-off right the more waves you'll catch and the more frequently you'll be in the best position to maximise your ride."

BOTTOM TURNS AND TOP TURNS

Introduction

You're off, dropping down the face of the wave, accelerating all the time. As you near the base of the wave you lean and edge hard, forcing your kayak to grip the water as you redirect that speed across the face of the wave. With the wave now peeling behind you you've a perfect smooth slope to play on. Drop down the slope, accelerate and bottom turn, rise up the slope, lose speed and top turn. If you adjust the timings of each to fit the ever changing characteristics of the wave the ride will just go on and on.

But have you ever thought about these turns: how they work, why they work, what choices you have and which one to select? You might have been surfing for years, be totally intuitive or you might be new to the sport; whatever your situation it won't hurt to stop for just a moment and review your options.

Bottom turns and top turns are the bread and butter of surfing. There's nothing particularly complicated about them but use the right turn in the right place at the right time and you could be a world champion! The terms 'bottom' and 'top' go a long way in creating a picture of the turns but in doing so they also restrict your imagination. I'd rather refer to high speed turns and low speed turns.

The classic high speed carving turn

The bottom turn is the classic high speed turn.
Imagine yourself at the very top of a six foot near vertical face. You've done all the hard work and the power of the wave is about to take over. Your fall down the face is like being in a lift when all the cables snap! You're propelled down the face by the force of gravity accelerating all the time. At the bottom of the face, with all this energy, turned to speed, it's time to redirect your run. But how? It's easy - ever heard of Wilf O'Reilly?

"Bottom turns and top turns are the bread and butter of surfing."

"Head and shoulders steady with eyes focused on the end of the turn."

Wilf O'Reilly

For those of you who haven't, let me paint the picture. Wilf, apart from doing the odd Heinz baked bean advert, was the British gold medal short track speed skating champion back in a distant Olympic games. You've heard of short track speed skating of course. Four skaters start together and sprint around a normal sized ice rink; the turns are sharp, fast and furious. The skaters carve their turns on the very inside edge of their skates. Head and shoulders steady with eyes focused on the end of the turn. Their bodies low and overhanging the ice, inside arm stretched out with just the flats of their hands skimming the smooth floor of the rink for balance.

Components and limitations

"Keep your body off the water by using the back of your paddle blade as a skimming outrigger."

And that's all there is to it. If you want to carve a high speed turn on a wave then think of nothing more than Wilf O'Reilly. Edge your boat hard on its inside rail, keep your head and shoulders steady, focusing on the end of the turn. Keep your body leaning forwards and overhanging the inside edge of your boat but keep it off the water by using the back of your paddle blade as a skimming outrigger. Dropping down the face of a steep wave will give you all the speed needed to power this turn. However, if you're in a fast kayak or ski then on the right shaped wave-face travelling at warp factor nine you might like to try performing a high speed carving turn at the top of the wave. It'll blow your mind!

The low speed pivot and skim turn

So what do you do at the top of a wave if you're not travelling like the USS Enterprise escaping from the Klingon empire? The answer is a low speed pivot and skim turn. Here speed is in short supply and being lost fast as you track up the face of the wave. Don't leave this turn too late. It's not called a no speed turn after all! You're losing speed fast so once you've decided to turn you'll need to turn and drop back down that sloping wave face as fast as possible or you can kiss this ride good-bye. Try carving a top turn at such low speed and you'll just trip over your nose.

The paddle-out take-off

Performing a paddle-out take-off is the perfect way of isolating a low speed pivot and skim turn and in white water waves it's relatively easy. Start from the shore and paddle out over a couple of waves. When you see the next powerful white water wave approaching carry on paddling towards it at about 45°. Just before you hit the wave pre-rotate your upper body towards the shore and get ready to unwind this pre-rotation during the turn. As the wave hits the nose of your boat it'll initiate a turn towards the beach. A sweep stroke on the seaward side of your boat or a mid boat pivot (a bit like a pry stroke in line with your hips) on the beachward side will sharpen and speed up the turn. Throughout this violent turn hold on to your good forward leaning body position; it's the only way to maintain stability. It'll also produce good trim and will stop the tail of your boat snagging in the white water half way through the turn. Get it right and your boat will want to skim sharply around with you facing back down the wave. Just minimise the resistance to the turn and you've got it.

"A sweep stroke on the seaward side of your boat or a mid boat pivot on the beachward side will sharpen and speed up the turn."

"During a paddle-out take-off or a low speed

pivot and skim top turn you need to be able to

hold a strong skimming edge."

Minimising resistance, thinking about skimming

So how do you minimise resistance for both the paddle-out take-off and the low speed pivot and skim turn. Think of trying to skim a stone as far as possible across a pool or bongo sliding a kayak for as long as possible in front of a wave. In both these cases and when you want to perform a low speed pivot and skim turn, you're setting the angle of the stone or hull at "Skim". Look at the way you hold that stone next time you skim it - the bottom of the stone is flat to the water, with the leading edge raised ever so slightly but just enough so that the stone doesn't trip over and plunge into the water. Experiment when you next bongo slide on a wave. For the longest skimming bongo slide you don't want to let the beachward edge of your boat catch or it's curtains! But equally, lift that edge too high and your skimming days are over due to too much resistance.

During a paddle-out take-off or a low speed pivot and skim top turn you need to be able to hold a strong skimming edge. This skimming position will allow the kayak to spin around without letting the beachward edge catch in still water. At the start of this turn it's the front of your kayak that's liable to snag. Lightening the nose by momentarily leaning back will decrease the chances of tripping over its beachward edge. However this position is unstable (too unstable to be used during the paddle-out take-off) and has a negative effect on trim, so as soon as the nose has passed through 90° quickly rock into a good forward body position, allowing the turn to develop.

Adaptations to the two models

The high speed carving turn and the low speed pivot and skim turn are two extreme examples but blend elements of each and you'll have a turn for every occasion. One of my favourites is a high speed turn at the top of the wave initiated by sudden body rotation and applied edge. This slashes the tail of the boat clean over the back of the wave, throwing spray even higher. It's like watching someone on a BMX bike skid their back wheel around and come to a halt, dust flying everywhere. Another favourite is the low speed pivot and skim performed in a high performance finned kayak at the very top of a breaking face. With critical judgement, this time the front of the kayak is clean out of the water. The kayak pivots around both paddle and its central fin as the lip of the wave pushes the kayak around and back down the wave face.

"There's plenty to think about, but unlocking that speed is part of the fun."

Your speed dictates your turn

Speed is the key: once you've got speed in excess you'll find the wave opening out in front of you, with endless possibilities. Surf boards, skis and surf kayaks have all attempted to maximise their speed potential. Compare the hull shape of any of these to a standard playboat and you'll see dramatic differences. The slope of a wave will affect speed. The trim of your craft will affect speed. Even the material your craft is made of will affect speed. Sure there's plenty to think about, but unlocking that speed is part of the fun.

"It's like watching someone on a BMX bike skid their back wheel around and come to a halt, dust flying everywhere."

*Mid-way through a classic pivot and skim
top turn in a high performance surf kayak.*

"It's not a sudden turn and it doesn't have to be at the bottom of a wave. In fact, with enough speed and a bowling wave face this is a great turn to execute at the top of a wave."

Summary

Referring to bottom turns and top turns is fine but in reality the type of turn you perform is determined by the speed you're travelling at. At low speeds your options are limited. If you're in a slow kayak tracking back up the wave face and losing speed fast then the only real option available is the low speed pivot and skim turn.

As your speed increases your options increase. At the bottom of a wave where you're generally travelling at high speeds you can execute a high speed carving turn. The better the edge of your kayak grips the water the less energy is lost and the more speed you'll carry around the turn. It's not a sudden turn and it doesn't have to be at the bottom of a wave. In fact, with enough speed and a bowling wave face this is a great turn to execute at the top of a wave.

At speeds in-between these two extremes there are variations and combinations of both. Tail slash top turns require speed and a parallel approach along the crest of the wave. A sudden hip flick and engagement of the inside edge will redirect the kayak to fall down the face. Faster kayaks will carry more speed to the very top of a wave and so the low speed pivot and skim turn can be performed higher and higher up the wave face until the nose of the kayak breaks free of the wave, producing big off-the lip turns.

* Think of your turns in terms of speed rather than their position at either the top or bottom of the wave.

* To carve a high speed turn think of the body position adopted by short track speed skaters as they carve around their turns in the ice.

* Performing a paddle-out take-off is the perfect way of isolating a low speed pivot and skim turn.

* During a low speed pivot and skim top turn you need to hold a strong skimming edge whilst powering the turn by unwinding your body's pre-rotation.

* Adaptations include the tail slash top turn and big off-the-lip turns

* As speed is the key to these turns so the design of your kayak will have a profound effect on what you can achieve.

MAKING THE SECTION

Introduction

Surfing across the face of a wave might seem like a simple enough technique but have you ever stopped for a moment and really thought about what is going on? Why can you surf right across the face of some waves whilst on others the only way you can keep up momentum is to surf straight towards the beach? Why do some surfers consistently make it through a fast close-out section whilst others always get caught by the breaking wave? Think about the forces involved, the design of your craft and your use of technique and you might just unlock the secret to making the very sections that have been a barrier in your past.

The aim of this chapter is to get you thinking about how you can make the most of this complex three dimensional environment and why we do the things we do.

Diagonal angle and angle of fall

In order to surf an unbroken wave you simply need to keep falling down the wave face faster than you are being pulled back up it. The notion that as we surf we're constantly fighting this pull is not always clear. But, whether you're surfing a stationary river wave or a moving ocean wave, the forces are the same.

★ Gravity will try and pull you down the wave face. This is fairly obvious.

★ The flow of water over the wave will try to pull you up and over that wave. This isn't so obvious, but if you picture a stationary river wave, with the current flowing up and over it, you'll get the idea. An ocean wave has exactly the same relationship between movement and flow except we see the wave moving and aren't so aware that this must cause a relative current to flow up and over the wave itself.

Thankfully the kayaks in which we surf are designed to offer the minimum resistance to this flow and so in most cases they are quite happy to let gravity pull them down the wave face. In fact, our kayaks have such low resistance that given a steep enough face we don't even have to fall straight down it. On a steep face we can set our kayaks to run diagonally down the wave. As a result of running at an angle down the face we consequently reduce the angle at which we fall.

If we simplify a wave face and imagine that it's a straight slope from top to bottom then it follows that as the angle of our diagonal run increases so the actual angle at which the kayak is falling (angle of fall) will decrease. At a specific diagonal angle (and therefore a specific angle of fall) the pull down of gravity will be perfectly resisted by the pull up of the current passing up and over the wave. At this critical angle an observer from the beach will see us surfing across

"Surfing across the face of a wave

might seem like a simple enough

technique but have you ever stopped

for a moment and really thought

about what is going on?"

the wave face but neither dropping or climbing. We'll be tracking perfectly level across the slope.

Changing the angle of our ride in relation to the critical diagonal angle will upset the balance of these two opposing forces. When we surf at an angle less than the critical diagonal angle we'll fall further down the wave face. When we surf at an angle greater than the critical diagonal angle we'll rise up the wave face, eventually being pulled off the wave altogether.

"When surfing across a steep wave we will be able

to maintain a larger diagonal angle than when

we're surfing across a shallow sloping wave."

Factors that will increase the critical diagonal angle

The critical diagonal angle will depend on many things but will be increased by factors that improve your ability to fall down the wave. These factors include the following:

* Materials and designs which produce low surface resistance between the kayak hull and the water.
* Design features that minimise other forms of resistance and drag.
* Good forward trim to minimise drag.
* Surfing as steep a wave as possible.
* Positioning yourself on the steepest part of the wave face. On a real wave face this is incredibly important as the face is not a simple slope but a curved slope that gets progressively steeper from the base of the face to the lip.

If we use the critical diagonal angle as a reference point then we can make the following general statements:

* When surfing across a steep wave we will be able to maintain a larger diagonal angle than when we're surfing across a shallow sloping wave.

* The critical diagonal angle is greater on a steep wave than on a shallow sloping wave. It's also greater on the steepest part of the wave's sloping face i.e. the top third of the wave face compared to the shallower sloping bottom third of the face.

* If we surfed exactly the same wave in a standard playboat and then again in a specifically designed surf kayak we'd find that the critical diagonal angle would be greater in the surf kayak. This is due to the design features of a surf kayak creating less resistance to forward movement than the playboat.

* On a steep wave face we will be able to hold both a large diagonal angle and a steep angle of fall resulting in a high speed ride across the wave face. A great example of this is when you're tracking along inside the barrel of a tubing wave. An observer on the beach might see you holding your vertical position as you zoom through the barrel but inside the wave you feel that in fact you're always surfing diagonally down the face.

Edging

So that's the theory but what about the practice? So far I've mentioned running diagonally across the wave face with no explanation at all about how this is achieved. I'm sure that many of you have got a fair idea but depending on the type of craft you paddle you might find that there are a couple of ways of achieving the same result.

What stops a kayak from skimming down a wave face straight towards the shore? It's not a new problem and in fact centuries ago sailing ships had a similar problem. The only difference to the question was "what stops a sailing ship from being constantly blown straight down wind?". A similar problem with a similar answer; both craft need to generate a keel. Sailing ships have theirs built into their hulls and as surf kayakists we generate ours by holding the edge of our kayaks into the face of the wave, a technique referred to as edging (if in any doubt as to which edge I mean, experiment, you'll soon find out).

For our kayaks to run diagonally across the slope of a wave we need to hold the seaward edge of the kayak into that wave. A hard edged position will eliminate wasted side slip and maximise forward momentum.

Factors that create an effective edge

A high degree of edge. If inside of our kayak we raise one knee slightly higher than the other we will cause our kayak to edge. To create a 'keel' effect we need to dip the seaward edge of our kayak into the wave face. We need to hold this edge at a relatively steep angle in the water if we want our kayak to grip the face. If we lessen the edge we risk our kayak sliding down the face.

Sharp, long and relatively straight edges along the stern of the kayak. Sharper edges slice deeper into the wave face for the same amount of edging compared to a rounded hulled boat, therefore increasing its relative grip. The longer the edge the better it will grip, and the straighter the edge the less turning effect compared to a highly curved edge as found on many playboats.

Addition of fins. If you surf a kayak with a thruster fin set up (three fins under the kayak) then imagine the two outside fins as extensions to the edge of the boat. The side fins will make the edge of your kayak even grippier; a useful extension of the kayak's edge and very useful when carving high speed turns.

"For our kayaks to run diagonally across the slope of a wave we need to hold the seaward edge of the kayak into that wave."

Running diagonally with or without the

"A clean cutting beachward rudder can be used to hold you straight or to generate a great deal of turning force with a negligible amount of additional drag."

beachward rudder

In modern surf kayaks the edge is so effective that we don't actually require that much knee lift in order to get it to bite or grip the wave face. Any kayak that has a long enough, sharp enough, straight enough stern edge can create an effective 'keel'. Edge harder and look up towards the top of the wave and you'll turn; you'll increase your diagonal angle and you'll move up the wave face. Lessen your edge and look towards the shore and you'll turn the other way; you'll decrease your diagonal angle and you'll drop down the wave face.

Other kayaks can also create a 'keel'. If these kayaks are rounded rather than edgy, highly rockered rather than flat, and short rather than long - then the keel that is created might need a little help from a beachward rudder. The 'keels' that these kayaks form by edging tend to turn the kayak up the wave. Turning up the wave can also be a product of body rotation. The use of a beachward rudder can help in both situations.

A paddle acting as a rudder on your beachward side can be used to turn your kayak towards the shore. A clean cutting beachward rudder can be used to hold you straight or to generate a great deal of turning force with a negligible amount of additional drag. Forces that turn you up the wave can be balanced by the effect of the beachward

rudder which wants to turn you down the wave. Balance these two opposing forces and you surf in straight diagonal line, across the wave face.

When experimenting with the use of a beachward rudder it's best to set your kayak on its edge and set the beachward rudder at the very start of a diagonal run. Changes in the relative forces applied to each can then be smoothly adjusted as the ride continues. Once edge and rudder are set, the angle of the diagonal run will need constant adjustments simply to maintain your position along the ever changing wave face gradient. Additional adjustments can be used to create rise and fall as you surf across the wave face.

★ To fall down the wave face and gain speed, look down the wave, push the rudder away from the kayak (increasing pressure on the outside of the blade) and decrease the amount of edge.

★ To climb up the wave face and lose speed, look up the wave, increase the degree of edge and decease rudder pressure.

Summary

We don't all think or indeed learn the same way and I'm sure that for some of you this chapter has taken a very long time to explain a very simple technique. However I'm equally sure that for some the process of thinking through these concepts will be useful. Making the section is all about maximising your speed across the wave face. But, different waves, different positions on the face and different boats will affect just how fast you can go. If you understand what it is you're trying to do then at least you can practise the right things. Once you get your technique and positioning in tune you'll be blasting across sections that in the past have blasted you.

* To run diagonally across the slope of a wave we need to hold our kayak's seaward edge into the wave.

* Any kayak that has a long enough, sharp enough, straight enough edge can create an effective 'keel'.

* Rounded, highly rockered and short kayaks can also create a 'keel' but its effectiveness will be enhanced with the use of a beachward rudder.

* Edge hard and look up towards the top of the wave and you'll turn up the wave face.

* Lessen your edge and look towards the shore and you'll drop down the wave face.

"Making the section is all about maximising

your speed across the wave face."

ADVANCED WAVE RIDING SKILLS

Introduction

At first I was going to call this chapter "Advanced Manoeuvres" and run through a list of such things as spins, cutbacks, floaters, aerials and tube riding. However the more I thought, the more I realised that a simple list of moves would be missing the point. In addition to having a competent set of skills, advanced wave riding requires two additional components. The first is the environment - as any well executed, slick manoeuvre is totally dependent on the characteristics of the wave. This includes bottom turns, top turns and the diagonal run just as much as the manoeuvres described in this chapter. The second component is your own ability to see, think and plan into the future. To be an advanced wave rider you need to have released your conscious mind from the here and now and be thinking about what's coming up next. Only then will you be able to be in exactly the right position to perform the very best manoeuvres at precisely the right time.

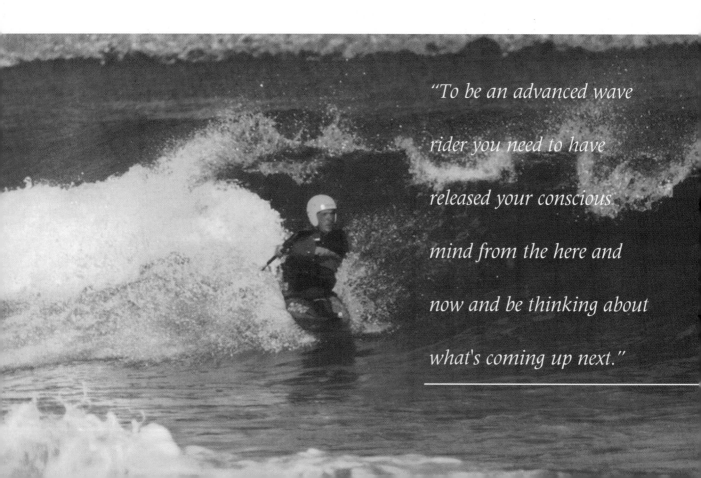

"To be an advanced wave rider you need to have released your conscious mind from the here and now and be thinking about what's coming up next."

Looking into the future

When we first learn a new skill we have to concentrate. In fact we concentrate to such a level on the elements of that skill that there's no thinking space left to concentrate on anything else. At first we can't even get the elements together; we're struggling and failing. Some people give up. But for those who keep trying, there's that wonderful experience when for the first time it clicks. We still need all our concentration, we're totally focused on the components of the skill to the exclusion of all else and if anything around us changes it'll be totally unexpected and will almost certainly lead to disaster!

My son, Zerran, is just learning to ride his bicycle. He's at the stage where he can pedal and balance but he can only do it successfully if he really concentrates hard. His conscious mind is totally engaged on performing the skill. He's learning to ride on our local cricket pitch which is big, flat and safe but it does have a fence around its perimeter. So what do you think Zerran does as he nears the edge of the pitch? Does he start to turn well in advance, smoothly banking his bike to turn away from the obstacle? Of course not: he doesn't even see the fence until it's too late, and then he doesn't even attempt to turn or stop. This change in the environment has come as a complete shock and he crashes straight into it.

Learning the skills of surfing is just like learning to ride a bike, except that we haven't got a nice flat cricket pitch on which to practise! The surfing environment is complex, turbulent and always changing. It's a tough place to learn and yet if we stick at it we will learn and develop complex new skills.

Over the years I've seen many of our local young self-taught board surfers developing their surfing skills. They progress from wiping out on every ride to the stage where they have managed to stand up for the first time. At first their concentration is 100% focused on the skills themselves and when the characteristics of the wave change it comes as an unexpected shock and they wipe out. But if they stick it out their wave riding ability improves - it gets more robust. As they start to learn what might happen to a wave during the course of a ride they also start to develop ways of dealing with these changes. They are still consciously controlling their skills but they've reached that point where their wave riding is competent (if still a little mechanical) and robust enough to deal with common environmental changes.

In the surfing environment it takes a long time to reach this conscious-of and robust stage and a long time is then spent at this stage before moving on. It often seems that the local board surfers get stuck at this stage for at least a season. During this time they are surfing more waves, dealing with more environmental changes and refining their skills accordingly. Then the second big click occurs. Having developed their skills to deal with all the minute and subtle changes as they're surfing across a wave they reach the point where they stop thinking about it. Conscious control becomes subconscious control and their minds become free to look into the future.

If we want to become more than just competent surfers then it's going to take time, effort and experience. However the rewards are well worth it. To be surfing with a free mind that is able to see and think and plan ahead will take our surfing to the next level. You don't actually need to be doing anything other than bottom turning, top turning and making the section. It's just that you'll be able to do all of them so much better.

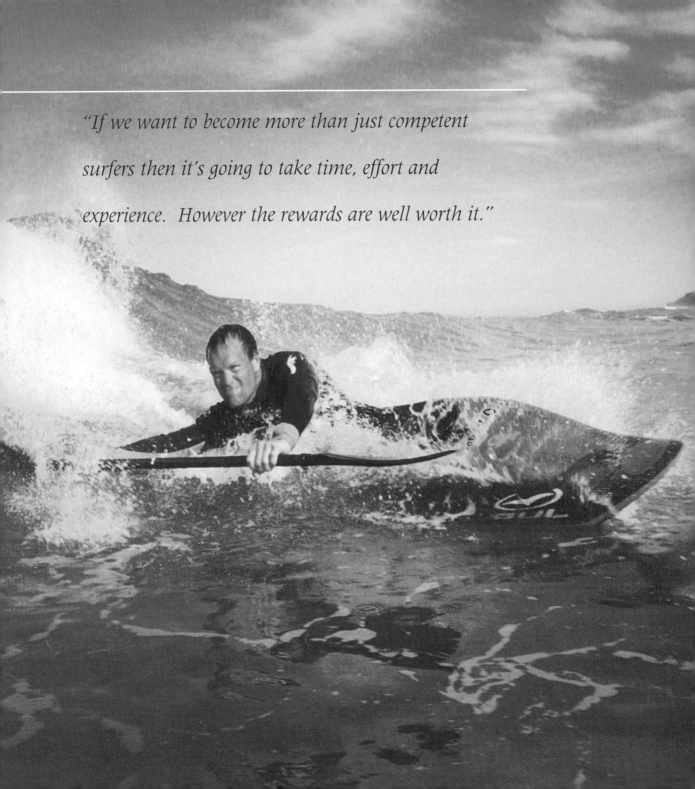

"If we want to become more than just competent surfers then it's going to take time, effort and experience. However the rewards are well worth it."

360° spins

360° or flat spins are a common sight these days.
Both surf kayaks and playboats have all the design features
necessary to allow this manoeuvre to be performed with
relative ease. In fact for some boats the question is not
so much how to flat spin as how not to! Take a boat with
a planing hull and sharp releasable rails (or edges) and you
have a boat that will spin. You can even add fins to it and
it'll still flat spin. All you then need is enough speed to get
you planing and a little bit of rotational force.

What makes flat spinning an advanced manoeuvre is
not so much the spin itself but where it's performed
and how it's finished. However it's a move that has a bad
name in the surf due to its over use, inappropriate use and
accidental use. But with a free mind and precise execution
it can be a daring move pulled off right in the depths of the
power pocket, and a move that will improve your
positioning on the wave face itself.

"What makes flat spinning an advanced manoeuvre is not so much the spin itself but where it's performed and how it's finished."

The key factor needed to switch on this manoeuvre is speed. Without speed you can push and sweep and twist as much as you like but your kayak won't spin. With speed you can initiate a flat spin almost anywhere on the wave face, falling down the face, at the bottom of the face even coming back up the face!

As long as you have speed all you need to do is create a rotational force, as you might do during a high speed carving turn, but don't engage your inside edge. Instead of hard edging, and therefore carving a turn, simply hold your kayak on a firm but lesser skimming edge and look where you want to go. Instantly the back end of your kayak will skim 180° around. Good body rotation, with your head and shoulders looking where you want to go, plus a subtle change of skimming edge will then pull the nose around completing the 360° spin.

With your subconscious mind controlling your surfing you'll spot the ideal position for this move. As long as you can avoid tying up your conscious mind during its execution you'll also be able to finish it facing in exactly the right direction to continue your ride.

The cutback

With your conscious mind free from your surfing you'll be able to see when a wave is likely to back off or when a fast, close out section is about to come to an end. You'll register that in just a moment's time you'll be surfing across a much shallower sloping wave face and that without any action your ride will slow down and possibly even come to a halt.

As you register this future event you might start to plan for a cutback. At this precise moment, however, you're travelling with speed across the wave face, running away from the ever chasing power pocket. As the wave backs off you'll hold on to this speed just long enough to be sent

further from the power pocket than you'd like. The trick is to use this speed to carve your first turn down the face of the wave and back towards the approaching power pocket.

As you drop down the face, at the start of this first turn, you'll gain a little bit extra speed; enough to propel you right back and up into the top corner of the power pocket. You're aiming to hit the approaching white water lip hard and high, and with speed. As you're approaching the white water lip of the power pocket you'll be coming off your first carving edge and about to engage your opposite edge in order to carve your second turn. This second turn is different as it'll start with you crashing into the white water

lip of the power pocket with the rest of the turn taking place in aerated white water. The crash gives you the opportunity to initiate a sudden change of direction, possibly as violent as a tail slash top turn or paddle-out take-off. The fall back down the turbulent and aerated white water needs to be carefully controlled to avoid over-rotation.

At the end of your descent down the white water lip you'll return with speed onto the green face of the wave right in the mouth of the power pocket ready, prepared and positioned for your next move. Cutbacks are used for more than just returning to the power pocket. In their own right they represent a well timed and complex sequence of moves which can include and combine the full spectrum of high speed carving and low speed pivot and skim turns, with pre-rotation during the second turn playing a vital role. The position gained after a cutback can be timed so as to lead straight into a tube ride or into a climb back up the wave face and top turn right in the mouth of the power pocket itself.

"a well timed and complex sequence of

moves which can include and combine

the full spectrum of high speed carving

and low speed pivot and skim turns"

The floater

Not so much a move as a well timed surfing line across the back of a breaking lip. As you're hurtling across the face of a wave you predict that ahead a section of the wave will break before you have a chance to get past it. You could attempt to skirt around in front of this section, simply pull over and off the wave, or set yourself up for a floater.

As you approach the closing out section, take a line diagonally down the wave face to pick up as much speed as possible. At the base of the face carve a long shallow high speed turn. Maintain your speed whilst aiming for the critical spot where you'll jump from the wave face onto the back of the breaking lip. Board riders really do jump at this point: watch them, watch their legs as they

"As you're hurtling across the face

of a wave you predict that ahead a

section of the wave will break before

you have a chance to get past it. "

spring up onto the back of the lip and then de-weight their boards as they float effortlessly across the breaking lip. This weighting/de-weighting of the board gives board riders a little more room for manoeuvre. Us poor old sit-down surfers have to hit the critical spot perfectly if we're to have any chance of floating over this section.

Once on the back of the lip it's almost all over. If we haven't already chosen the right line then we'll either end up off the back of the wave or worse, crashing down with the lip. If, however, we've chosen a good line and have enough speed we'll skim over this frictionless surface until we fall off its far end and re-engage with the wave face.

Take the approach for a floater, add a little more speed, make the wave face steeper and the lip sharper and you've got everything you need for an aerial. The biggest difference between this and a floater is your body position and the line you're following as you hit the lip.

Aerials, like all advanced manoeuvres, need a wave with just the right set of characteristics. But finding the right wave for an aerial is difficult. Basically you're looking for a fast peeling wave along which you encounter a peel from the opposite direction. Hitting the near breaking lip of this oncoming peel at exactly the right moment with enough speed to get airborne is incredibly hard. It shouldn't be any surprise that it's the approach that needs most time to get right.

Aerials

As you hit the vertical, near breaking lip ensure that your hull is flat relative to the surface of the slope. You want maximum speed, and edging here will just slow you down. Just as with the floater, the angle that you hit the lip will dictate your chances of success. Aim too vertically and you'll stall in mid air and fall back stern first. Aim too low and you won't get airborne at all. Get it just right for your speed and the characteristics of the wave, and you'll follow a natural arc through the air. Whilst airborne twist your trunk to reposition the kayak for a smooth landing.

A variation of this involves using your inside paddle to create extra lift at the moment of take off. Approach the lip in the same way as before but as you hit the lip give a sharp dig with your inside paddle at the very top of the wave. Leave the paddle in the wave as you and your kayak become airborne. This will not only lighten the load but will also give you contact with the wave, which can be useful for a mid-air turn and repositioning for landing.

"Aerials like all advanced manoeuvres need a wave with just the right set of characteristics but finding the right wave for an aerial is difficult."

"It's an experience not to be missed, screaming along, truly inside the barrel with every chance of actually making it out again. For me it's got to be the ultimate experience."

Tube riding

Needing the right sort of wave is obvious. A peeling wave that is breaking in such shallow water that, as the lip is breaking, it is thrown forwards creating a hollow tube between the falling lip and the face of the wave. The first trick is getting into this tube; the second trick is getting out of it!

In my own experience I've come across two quite different situations where I've become tubed. In the first situation getting tubed is almost coincidental to your plans: in the second getting tubed is your main priority, requiring a precise approach and execution.

For the first situation picture yourself surfing across the face of a fast peeling wave. Your speed across this face is limited by your position on the wave face and the characteristics of the wave (see chapter 8). However the speed at which the wave peels is in direct relation to the underwater shape of the beach. If you're surfing across the face as fast as you can but the wave is peeling even faster, then sooner or later it'll catch you up or even over take you. If you're lucky the peeling wave may be creating a tube which, as it catches you, swallows you up whole. But it's not over yet. As long as you adapt your ride, maximise your forward trim, adjust your line to fall diagonally down the face you might create just enough extra speed to escape this tubing section and carry on for the rest of your ride.

When getting tubed is my primary goal I've found a combination of a hard bottom turn and mid-face top turn does the trick. Combining these turns has the effect of initially losing speed across the wave face (stalling) and then repositioning you on a fast line so enabling you to make it through the tube.

Start by falling straight down the wave face (often from the take-off itself), leave your bottom turn later than normal but then make it as sharp as possible. As you start to climb back up the face re-align yourself on a fast line across the wave face by means of a pivot and skim top turn (see chapter 7). Perform this combination just as a section of the wave is about to tube and you'll find yourself instantly inside the barrel. Leave your pivot and skim top turn too late and you'll end up too high on the wave face getting sucked over with the tubing lip! Perform it too low and the pitching lip will land on your head! Get it right and instantly re-align to the perfect fast escape line, diagonally down the face of the wave and you're there. It's an experience not to be missed, screaming along, truly inside the barrel with every chance of actually making it out again. For me it's got to be the ultimate experience.

Summary

There's more to advanced surfing than just increasing the list of manoeuvres that you can perform. It's all about freeing your conscious mind from concentrating on the immediate action of surfing, allowing it to look into the future and plan for what's going to happen next. Once your mind is working ahead of your actions you'll be able to perform your skills in more critical parts of the wave, achieving more spectacular results. Flat spins just require speed and rotation, a cutback is just a well timed and well positioned sequence of turns. Floaters and aerials require a precise approach towards a difficult target and tube riding requires adjustments to a normal bottom-turn top-turn combination.

* To be an advanced wave rider you need to have released your conscious mind from the here and now and be thinking about what's coming up next.

* What makes flat spinning an advanced manoeuvre is not so much the spin itself as where it's performed and how it's finished.

* Cutbacks represent a well timed sequence of moves which can include and combine the full spectrum of high speed carving and low speed pivot and skim turns.

* The floater is not so much a move as a well timed surfing line across the back of a breaking lip. It's more difficult in a kayak than on a board due to the fact that we can't jump or de-weight our craft.

* For an aerial take the approach for a floater, add a little more speed, make the wave face steeper and then make the lip sharper.

* When getting tubed is your primary goal, carve a late hard bottom turn followed by a mid-face top turn.

"Once your mind is working ahead of your actions you'll be able to perform your skills in more critical parts of the wave, achieving more spectacular results."

TERMINOLOGY

The general environment

Swell

The wave or waves before they are steep enough to be ridden. Surfers often talk about the 'quality of the swell', its size, the distance it's travelled and how local wind conditions are affecting it.

Sets

A set of waves is a group of larger waves that will approach the shore at fairly regular intervals. The number of waves in a set, the time between sets and the precise pattern of waves in a set will be fairly stable during a specific surfing session.

Inside, Outside and the Line-Up

These are areas rather than parts of an actual wave but worth noting. The line-up or impact zone is the area in which the waves tend to break. Bigger waves will tend to break further out to sea and the line-up tends to be associated with these bigger or set waves. Outside is anything further out to sea, beyond the line-up. You might hear a fellow surfer in the line-up shouting "outside" when they see a huge set of waves appearing on the horizon. This is a good time to either start paddling further out to sea or back to the beach, depending on your ability and courage! Inside is anywhere shoreward of the main breaking waves. Sometimes waves will break more than once as they approach the shore. The first break will be referred to as the outside break, with subsequent breaks referred to as inside breaks.

Take-Off Zone and Take-Off Spot

Much the same as the line-up, the take-off zone is an area where waves consistently start to break and an area around which surfers will wait for their next ride.
The take-off spot is the optimum position within this zone to catch a wave - usually a position where the wave is at its very steepest just before breaking. Obviously these positions are not fixed and will be adjusted by each wave and the movement of the tide. Along the path of a long peeling wave there will be several possible take-off spots. However surfers catching the wave earliest in its break will have priority.

Swell

Sets

Inside, Outside and the Line-Up

Take-Off Zone and Take-Off Spot

Anatomy of a wave

White Water Waves

Lots of names for these: the broken wave, the soup, the pile and often referred to as the Inside. White water waves are not all the same. Some form quickly with a huge explosion of energy and then die away to nothing, whilst others roll in for hundreds of metres slowly losing energy as they approach the shore. A very useful type of wave for practising skills, manoeuvres and judgement.

Wave Face

The unbroken part of a wave that is steep enough to be surfed. The wave face will be at its steepest right next to where the wave is breaking. This area is often referred to as the power pocket. As you move away from the power pocket the slope of the wave face decreases until a point where it is too shallow for a surfer to ride.

Green Wave

An unbroken wave or the part of the wave that is unbroken. Surfers refer to surfing a green wave in order to separate it from a broken or white water wave.

Power Pocket

This is the steepest and therefore most powerful part of the wave face found closest to where the wave is breaking and associated with a peeling wave.

The Lip

The top edge of the wave that is about to break or is actually breaking. Off-shore winds will increase the steepness of the lip before it breaks, resulting in it being more powerful and well defined. On-shore winds cause waves to break with a shallow sloping face, resulting in a less powerful lip that spills down the wave.

Peeling Wave

A wave that, after breaking at a given point, continues to break along its length in a progressive way. Waves peel at different rates and it's this rate of peeling that needs to be matched by the speed of the surfer travelling across its face.

Closing Out

This is when a whole wave breaks suddenly or in a single instant, denying the surfer the opportunity to surf across its face.

Backing Off

This is the result of a steep or broken wave encountering deep water. The action of a wave breaking goes into reverse; the wave loses energy and steepness turning back into a low powered, shallow sloping swell.

White Water Waves

Wave Face

Green Wave

Power Pocket

The Lip

Peeling Wave

Closing Out

Backing Off

Section

Backing Off Section

Fast or Good Section

Bowling Section

Hollow, Cover-Up or Tubing Section

Close-Out Section

Sections of a wave

Section

A section is encountered as you surf across a peeling wave. There are various types of section that require a change of surfing technique and provide opportunities for the surfer to exploit.

Backing Off Section

The wave face loses steepness and power; a good place for cutbacks.

Fast or Good Section

The wave face gets steeper and more powerful. This might be time to gun it, holding a fast and high diagonal line just to get past this section as quickly as possible. Alternatively it might be an opportunity for a huge top turn or off-the-lip.

Bowling Section

This is a real interesting one: rare, but easy to recognise. This fantastically steep section of the wave face appears to wrap in on itself forming the inside side of a bowl. A long bottom turn as you enter this bowl will maintain your speed to such an extent that as you hit the lip you'll be able to pull an inverted carving top turn and get the feeling that you're travelling at warp factor 9!

Hollow, Cover-Up or Tubing Section

No surprises here. The wave has just encountered a sudden shallow ledge or sand bank causing the wave face to hollow out, throwing the lip of the wave shorewards. There might just be enough time to set yourself up on a diagonal track before you're surfing inside this watery barrel; keep your head down and hope you'll make it.

Close-Out Section

As you approach this section it may well look like a cover-up or tubing section. However this part of the wave is going to break in one sudden moment with hardly any chance of getting under the lip and continuing your ride. There's a lot of energy here, so be careful. There's no shame in bottling out and running for the shore. With courage it's a section that you could traverse with a floater or use for a spectacular end move or aerial.

Wind

On-shore, Cross-shore and Off-shore

These phrases refer to wind direction in relation to the specific break you're surfing.

Cross-Shore

Light cross-shore winds aren't a problem especially when you surf across a wave with the wind behind you. However surf the other way and you'll soon get fed up of being blinded by the constant spray in your face. As cross-shore winds increase they start to blow you along a beach and towards potential danger. In these conditions it can be really hard, if not impossible, to stay in a fixed, safe position in the water.

On-shore

Although we need wind to generate the swell in the first place, it's best if you don't also have that wind blowing straight onto the beach when you're surfing. On-shore winds push waves over before they would normally break. This will limit the steepness of rideable wave faces which therefore decreases surfing speed. Because the waves are breaking earlier, there's also more white water to get through; sometimes you'll see white water to the horizon! The wind itself will also make it a lot harder to paddle out.

Off-shore

It might sound strange but the best wind direction for surfing is a light off-shore wind blowing in the opposite direction to the surf. A light off-shore wind will hold up a wave face, causing it to get steeper than normal before it breaks. This is great news for the experienced surfer as this extra steepness means even more speed. However there are some negatives. Off-shore winds can make it harder to catch a wave as you're constantly being blown backwards whilst you try to take-off. Falling fast down the face of a steep wave ought to be exhilarating but in off-shore conditions the spray created at the front of your kayak can be blinding. On a larger scale, a strong continuous off-shore wind will eventually flatten any approaching swell and send it in the opposite direction.

On-Shore, Cross-Shore and Off-Shore

Cross-Shore

On-Shore

Off-Shore

Features caused by the shape of the seabed

Rips, Gutters and Channels

No beach or sea bed is a simple slope into the ocean. Variations in the shape of the bed will not just have an effect on the shape of the incoming wave but will also have an effect on how water from the broken waves drains back into the ocean. Have a look at a beach or break at low tide and you'll be able to see the low spots. When the tide comes in and the surf is breaking these low spots will channel the returning water back to the ocean forming rips, gutters or channels. Rips, gutters and channels are really all the same thing: deep areas where the water and therefore a current is moving out to sea. Because these channels are deeper than the seabed around them, waves will tend to back-off as they pass over them.

Gutters

Gutters tend to direct water across a beach and into a rip or channel.

Rips

A rip is often identified as a danger to swimmers because the current will pull swimmers out of their depth and into deeper water. A lifeguard may classify rips into several categories, all generally associated with sandy beaches and all having the same effect.

Channel

A channel tends to be a more positive term used by surfers to identify the deep water, seaward following current which is a useful means of getting out to the line-up without having to encounter the full force of the breaking surf. Channels are often associated with rocky sea beds, river mouths, point breaks and reef points.

Beach Break

The type of surf you'll see off a sandy beach - the waves break as they encounter the shallow sloping beach or sand banks. The power of the breaking waves will be affected by the slope of the beach and will change as the shape of the beach changes. Shallow sloping beaches will cause waves to break in a progressive spilling style whilst steep sided sand banks or a steep section of the beach will cause waves to break suddenly in a dumping, close-out or tubing manner.

Point Break

Where a headland juts out into the ocean. Oncoming waves will first encounter the end of the headland and will break at this point. As the wave continues to make its way along the headland more and more of the wave will break. Point breaks create peeling waves, the features of which depend on the precise shape of the seabed around the headland, the tide and the various qualities of the swell. A point break will provide predictable rides during a session.

Rips, Gutters and Channels

Gutters

Rips

Channel

Beach Break

Point Break

Reef Break

There's usually a good channel to aid getting you back out but be careful if you get caught inside, as there's often rocks and boulders lurking in the shallows.

Reef Break
Where a rocky shelf or a coral reef suddenly causes the seabed to become shallow. As waves encounter this sudden decrease in depth the bottom of the wave slows down whilst the lip of the wave is thrown forwards, causing the wave to tube. When the right shaped reef combines with a swell from the right direction peeling, tubing waves are the result. Reef breaks provide predictable, often very fast, rides with good channels for getting back out. Be careful; the speed of these rides takes some getting used to and wiping out over a shallow reef can be a painful and indeed life threatening experience.

I would never have written this book if it were not for the support and encouragement I've had from my family and friends since I first jumped into a leaky old scout kayak on the Bude Canal. From those early days I must specifically thank my dad Michael Hammond, my first kayak coach Bill Cook and best mate Shane White, who dragged me into many early adventures. From my teenage years and beyond I must thank Sam Roberts who was an inspiration as both a coach and as a surfer. Thanks to Andrew Hawker who gave me my first chance to surf for England and to Pete, Pete, Gary and James who made my first trip to a World Championships so memorable. Thanks to my father-in-law Nick Cole for his years of advice and support, to Paul Hurrell for pushing me to get started and who together with Bryce and Eggy were part of my incredible experience of becoming a World Champion. Thanks to Peter Knowles for his professional help in producing this book and to Sam Taylor for her fantastic book design. I'd also like to thank Lendal, Mega Kayaks, Gul International and Gecko Headgear for their support and to Richard Ward, Kayakojacko, Paul Hurrell and Kent Ford for their kind words. Most of all I'd like to thank my wonderful wife Nicola and sons Keiran and Zerran for the time I've spent in the surf and the time it's taken to compile this book.

Acknowledgements

Photo credits

This book would be nothing without the 90 photographs within its pages. Getting the right image for the right part of the book was no easy job and would have been impossible were it not for the many people around the world that sent in images for me to use. Thank you to everyone who responded to my pleas for help.

I'd particularly like to thank the following people for their contributions.

Iain Armstrong for the cover photo taken at Summerleaze Beach as I hit a rebound wave off the wall of our sea pool which threw me up into the air.

Ewart Aylward for some great shots and a particularly beautiful shot which we've used to start off chapter 5.

Jonny Bingham and **Dessie McGlinchey** who sent me the Northern Irish Surf Team collection. I've used many of these images, including a great shot of how difficult it can be to launch a kayak from a rocky shore, chapter 5.

Jason Birt, **Steve Bowens** and **Dan Sollom** whose photos have been used extensively. They include a great cover up shot and the images at the start of chapters 1 and 4.

Nick Cole whose experiments one summer's evening produced the punch through sequence included in chapter 5.

Pete Cropper who gave me several prints a long time ago, including the double page image of Kenny King, chapter 4.

John Donnelly who recorded much of the action at the 2003 World Championships and whose images include double page spreads in chapters 2, 5 and 6.

Nathan Eades for a photo that almost got lost but tells a thousand words about slow speed top turns and is included in chapter 7.

Nicola Hammond for patiently taking photos to order and in doing so took some wonderful shots, including the shoreline at Thurso in chapter 1.

Jem Howe for providing me with some very specific images of him and his ski, and providing the book with other great images of ski riding.

Paul Hurrell who surfed with me one sunny day and with a crap camera shot some brilliant photographs, the best of which is in chapter 9.

Darren Joy who sent me hundreds of great images, the best of which has to be of the Aerial in chapter 9.

Andy Spink who provided the image for the contents page and other great shots, including those in chapters 8 and 9.

The photographs were chosen primarily to fit the text and then, where ever possible, to create variety. In some cases I had very little choice whereas in others I was swamped with great examples. I'm sorry if I didn't choose yours.

Biography

World Champion **Simon Hammond** first started surf kayaking as a young member of his local scout troop in Bude, North Cornwall. Simon still remembers those early days where he and his friends spent more time swimming than kayaking!

As a young boy Simon watched paddlers competing in slalom kayaks and shoes but his first surf craft turned out to be an Australian designed Raider surf ski. He has a passion for most sports and as a teenager enjoyed surfing, rock climbing and rugby. But it was on a ski that he showed his real potential by reaching the finals of the English Open in his very first competition.

Simon and his wife Nicola returned to Bude after their college years and took over the family business Shoreline Outdoor Pursuits. As the business has developed so has their coaching experience with Simon now coaching outdoor pursuits and teaching physical education at the local school.

A return to surf competition in the late 90s coincided with Simon developing as a top BCU level 5 surf kayak coach. During his trip to the 2001 Worlds in Santa Cruz he recognised the qualities that made Kenny King World Champion. On the West coast of Ireland in 2003 it was a very focused and confident Simon Hammond that won heat after heat on his own way to becoming the world number one.

Simon is a regular contributor of articles to the canoeing press and this is his first book.

Simon Hammond